BRITISH ARMY CAP
BADGES OF THE FIRST
WORLD WAR

SHIRE PUBLICATIONS

BRITISH ARMY CAP BADGES OF THE FIRST WORLD WAR

PETER DOYLE AND CHRIS FOSTER

SHIRE PUBLICATIONS

Published in Great Britain in 2010 by Shire Publications Ltd, Midland House, West Way, Botley, Oxford OX2 0PH, United Kingdom.

44-02 23rd Street, Suite 219, Long Island City, NY11101, USA.

E-mail: shire@shirebooks.co.uk   ·   www.shirebooks.co.uk

A CIP catalogue record for this book is available from the British Library.

Shire Collections no. 6   ·   ISBN-13: 978 0 74780 797 1.

Peter Doyle and Chris Foster have asserted their right under the Copyright, Designs and Patents Act, 1988, to be identified as the authors of this book.

Designed by Ken Vail Graphic Design, Cambridge, UK and typeset in Bembo.

Printed in China through Worldprint Ltd.

10 11 12 14 15   10 9 8 7 6 5 4 3 2 1

COVER IMAGE
Typical infantry badges of the First World War.

PAGE 2 IMAGE
Soldier of the Royal Field Artillery in *c.* 1917, his cap badge modified to fit his fashionably soft 'trench cap'.

DEDICATION
For Julie, James and Sari.

ACKNOWLEDGEMENTS

We are indebted to Dorrien Thomas, who gave free access to his extensive badge collection; most of the Yeomanry badges illustrated in this book are his. Other friends provided images, information or badges themselves; they include Richard Archer, Bella Bennett, Brian Casterton, Barrie Duncan, Paul Evans, Muriel Hargraves, Chris Harrison, Alan Jeffreys, Robbie Leigh, Laurie Milner, John Richardson, David Smith, Julian Walker and Steven Wheeler. We are grateful to Nick Wright for his support; the membership of the Great War Forum for information and advice; and Peter Francis of the Commonwealth War Graves Commission for information on the design of CWGC headstones. Special mention must be made of Tom and Pete Halpin of the Merseyside Collectors Centre, for it was from Tom's market stall, several decades ago, that the first of the badges illustrated here was purchased.

PICTURE ACKNOWLEDGEMENTS

Permissions to reproduce pictures in this book have kindly been granted by:

Alan Williams of the Fovant Badges Society, page 28; Katy Iliffe, Sedburgh School archivist, for the images from Sedgwick House, pages 47, 67, 80, 102, 104, and 119; John Wainwright for the Bedfordshire Yeomanry, page 62; Tim Thurlow for his image of the R.N.D. Machine Gun Battalion, page 91; Geoff and Muriel Hargraves, pages 6 and 70; South Lanarkshire Council Museum Department for the image of the 5th Cameronians, page 96; Chris Harrison for his image of the Manchester Pals' Badge, page 108; and Richard Archer for his Women's Legion badge, page 124.

CONTENTS

PREFACE

THE FASCINATION with the British involvement in the First World War extends to all aspects of the conflict: the battles and their outcomes; the armies and their leaders; the conditions of trench warfare; and the controversies. All form part of a growing literature that examines every aspect of a war that has cast its shadow deeply.

A growing number of people interested in the conflict do so through a family connection. Medals, photographs and cap badges are the most common relics of a war that has all but died in living memory. Identification of cap badges on faded photographs is a first, important step in unravelling the military service of an individual. Then, as today, the cap badge was the British Army's most easily identifiable insignia. It represents a distillation of the pride of the regiment, its various battle honours and symbols borne proudly on the metallic emblem that was worn on all headdress, even within the trenches.

The purpose of this book is to describe and illustrate, for the historian and collector alike, the main types of badges used by the British Army in the First World War. This includes the main units that saw action; limited space precludes mention of the peripherals, such as the Volunteer battalions and the Officer Training Corps, but the majority of other corps and units, such as the 'Pals' battalions', the Royal Naval Division and the Territorial battalions, are included. Wherever possible, we have tried to illustrate genuine badges, though recognising fakes and forgeries is becoming an ever more difficult task. As space allows, we have also included images of the soldiers themselves wearing the badges. We hope this book provides a reference guide for all who wish to know more about the British Army of the Great War, and the actions of their relations in a war that has now faded from living memory.

Peter Doyle
Chris Foster

Left:
Cast bronze dish with the insignia of the Royal Engineers, one of the most populous of the corps of the British Army of 1914.

Opposite:
Lance-corporal Harry Hargraves of the Duke of Wellington's (West Riding Regiment), pictured in c. 1917. He survived the war; his brother John would be less fortunate.

Chapter One

THE BRITISH SOLDIER

T HE BRITISH ARMY has a venerable history. At its heart is the regiment, with its distinctive ceremonials, regimental colours, mottoes and mascots intended to propagate *esprit de corps*, marrying the British soldier to his parent unit, thereby creating loyalty in battle. While much of the mechanics of *esprit de corps* is intangible, pervading the ethos of regimental depots, or is unapproachable and reverential, such as the colours laid up in churches and cathedrals up and down the country, there remain those small metallic reminders of centuries of proud history, regimental cap badges.

Drawing on a badge tradition that stretches back to the identifying devices of the medieval feudal system, and springing from a long line of eighteenth- and nineteenth-century military fashions, the cap badge represents a distillation of the

The colours of the 1st Battalion, Duke of Wellington's West Riding Regiment, laid up in Halifax parish church. Originally the pride of the regiment, colours were last carried into battle in the late nineteenth century. The cap badge is a distillation of the same regimental traditions.

military history of the regiment or corps. In the age of uniform khaki, the language of the cap badge was there to be read by recruit and civilian alike; it remains today as one of the most potent symbols of military engagement through the centuries.

THE BRITISH ARMY

From medieval times the English and Scottish armies were formed of volunteers, raised by monarchs and feudal leaders. Though compelled to serve at times of emergency, gathered in local militias or trained bands, they were individual in spirit and appearance.

This individuality was swept away with Oliver Cromwell's New Model Army of May 1645, which marked the beginning of the modern regular army. Though it was formally disbanded during the Restoration of Charles II, many of the regiments of the New Model Army were taken into the King's service. Over time new corps were added to the military roster at times of national emergency; these would begin the formation of the amalgam that is the nation's army today. Yet the British Army proper was born following the Union of the English and Scottish parliaments in 1707. In the century after the Union, this new army was deployed across the world. The victories of the Duke of Marlborough over the French in the early eighteenth century, far-flung campaigns in four continents in the latter part of that century, and the pivotal battles of the Napoleonic War in the early part of the nineteenth century, culminating in the victory at Waterloo in 1815, were all to gild the achievements of British regiments. The Victorian wars that followed would bring mixed fortunes: the Crimea, which exposed weaknesses in army logistics; the Victorian 'small wars' over a variety of foes; and, at the close of the nineteenth century, the Second Boer War, fought against a determined, irregular but well-equipped force. These campaigns would nevertheless contribute honours that would become incorporated into regimental insignia.

The regimental system so pivotal to the British Army was developed in the late seventeenth century. Then, the regiment was a working business, raised and led by its Colonel and attracting monies from the state. Regiments bore the Colonel's name and carried insignia, flags known as 'colours', upon which were represented his arms, badges and mottoes. Very few of these devices survived a cull in the middle of the eighteenth century, when, by Royal Warrant, the arms and insignia of the colonels were removed and their names struck from titles in favour of a new system of numbered regiments of foot (the Infantry) and horse (the Cavalry). Precedence – the date of raising – determined the number applied and their position in the line.

A further dramatic change occurred in 1881, with infantry reforms by Lord Cardwell, then Tory Secretary of State for War, and his Liberal successor, Hugh C. E. Childers, which created the county regiments. Before the reforms, there were 109 regular infantry regiments. After, those regiments numbered from twenty-five onwards were paired, producing sixty-one in total, each with two regular battalions allied with a county or region, and each given a home depot. Militia and Volunteer battalions, part-time

Gale & Polden postcard from the early war period, illustrating the badge heritage of the Northamptonshire Regiment, formed from the linking of the 48th (Northamptonshire) and 58th (Rutland) Regiments of Foot in 1881.

THE NORTHAMPTONSHIRE REGIMENT

Officer's Embroidered Badge, 1860

Helmet Plate, 1860

Right: Cap badge worn between 1899 and 1908 by the 1st Volunteer Battalion, The Duke of Cornwall's Light Infantry. Volunteer battalions were an answer to the perceived threat from France, raised mostly in 1859. These battalions were to form the basis of the new Territorial Force in 1908.

Below: Cap badges of the Territorial regiments: Herefordshire, Hertfordshire, Monmouthshire, and Cambridgeshire.

Below right: Territorial soldier of the Royal Field Artillery. Volunteered for overseas service, he wears an Imperial Service badge on his right breast.

units with a long history of service, were also linked to these county regiments. A small consequence of the reforms was the stripping of numbers from regimental insignia; from this point on local devices, often associated with the location of their regimental depot, would replace them. The cavalry were not to suffer a similar fate until 1922, with a reduction in units following the experience of the First World War.

A further set of army reforms took place in 1908, instigated by a new Secretary of State for War, Lord Haldane, who announced the birth of the Territorial Force. With Haldane, each infantry regiment gained, in addition to its regular battalions, a third, Special Reserve, battalion (transferred from the Militia), its sole purpose to gather recruits for the regular battalions. The fourth, fifth and sixth battalions of a regiment were Territorial battalions, born of the Volunteer battalions that were raised in 1859, responding to threats from the Continent. Like the Volunteer battalions, the Territorial battalions were locally raised, and under the control of county Territorial associations, who managed recruitment through drill halls in different parts of each county. Irish regiments (as the whole of Ireland was then part of the United Kingdom) was never to have Territorial battalions.

Though most Volunteer battalions evolved into Territorial battalions of the county regiments following Haldane's reforms, others were transformed as a result of technological innovation – the development of the bicycle – into Territorial cyclists; new Cyclist battalions were also raised, with the bicycle wheel unsurprisingly forming the basis of their insignia. In addition, there were five all-Territorial

regiments: the multi-battalion County of London Regiment (distinct from the Royal Fusiliers, or City of London Regiment), and the Herefordshire, Hertfordshire, Monmouthshire and Cambridgeshire regiments, created from the amalgamation of local Volunteer battalions. The intention was that the part-time Territorials would be used for home defence in time of conflict; with the outbreak of the First World War in 1914, most volunteered for overseas service.

Enamel badge issued to the men of the 1st, 2nd and 3rd Birmingham City Battalions – the 14th, 15th and 16th (Service) Battalions, The Royal Warwickshire Regiment, in lieu of uniform in 1914.

The Yeomanry regiments, based mostly in the Shires, became the cavalry of the new force. Many of the Yeomanry regiments could trace their origins back to the late eighteenth century, when they had been raised to counter threats from the Continent; some were added to the force as further threats required, including during the Boer War. Others formed a Special Reserve for the regular Cavalry. In addition to Yeomanry and Infantry, the Territorial Force included units of the main support arms and services, with Territorial Gunners, Engineers, Royal Army Medical Corps, Army Service Corps, and so on, all taking their roles in the Territorial divisions.

Field Marshal Earl Kitchener of Khartoum took over as Secretary of State for War in August 1914. Understanding that the war would be costly in manpower, and that the eighty-four regular infantry battalions available at home – and seventy-three overseas – would be inadequate in a world war of unknown duration, Kitchener made a direct appeal to the public for sufficient men to support the war effort. Recruited initially via the Special Reserve system, 'Kitchener's Army' would grow from the avalanche of 'City' and Pals' battalions that were to be raised, the first in Liverpool, of men with similar backgrounds and circumstances. These were soon assimilated into the military machine as 'Service' battalions, numbered after the regular, Special Reserve and Territorial battalions of each county regiment.

The regular battalions available at home in 1914 were to form six infantry divisions; each division was to have three infantry brigades – with each brigade in turn composed of four infantry battalions (later reduced to three following the manpower shortage that was beginning to bite in 1917). Brigades rarely had more than one battalion from any one regiment, and a typical division would have men wearing very different cap badges. The infantry division of 1914 had a significant artillery presence, an attached cavalry squadron, and components from all the other service arms and support services to keep the division operating in the field – a massive undertaking with around fifteen thousand men in a typical full-strength division.

The six original divisions were to form the British Expeditionary Force (BEF) in 1914, the first four of them taking part in the Retreat from Mons in 1914, the other two being present in France by September 1914. The British Army grew in size to seventy-five infantry divisions, sixty-five of which would serve overseas as an effective fighting force, distributed between the various corps and armies engaged on all fronts. Of these, twelve would be regulars, one would be raised from Royal Naval reservists (the Royal Naval, later 63rd Royal Naval, Division), thirty would be 'New Army', raised originally from volunteers during Kitchener's direct appeal to the public in 1914–15, and the remainder would be Territorials. All would wear distinctive cap badges.

Right: Divisional signs. Top: 9th (Scottish) Division; 21st Division; 30th Division; 37th Division. Bottom: 40th Division; 52nd (Lowland) Division; 55th (West Lancashire) Division; 74th (Yeomanry) Division.

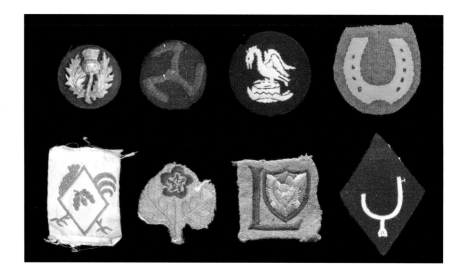

Below left: Seasoned soldiers of the Essex Regiment. All three wear soft 'trench caps' with Essex Regiment badges; the first soldier on the left wears a simplified uniform jacket; the others wear standard Service Dress. Inverted chevrons are good conduct badges indicating two years' good conduct; the single vertical stripe worn by the man in the centre was awarded for a single wounding. This man was also awarded the Military Medal.

Below: Wartime Service Dress. Left to right: Private, The Norfolk Regiment; Corporal, The Honourable Artillery Company (Infantry), with one year's overseas service chevron; Staff Sergeant, Royal Inniskilling Fusiliers, with two years' overseas service chevrons; and Staff Sergeant (Signaller Instructor), Royal Field Artillery, with four overseas service chevrons, and a single wounded stripe.

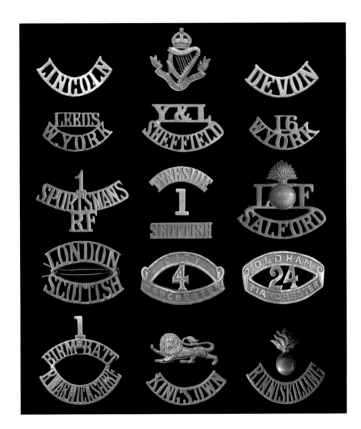

Above: Other ranks' collar badges. Top: Collar badges worn by all ranks of the 12th (Bermondsey) Battalion, the East Surrey Regiment – a Pals' battalion raised by the Mayor of Bermondsey in May 1915. Centre: Paired pick and rifle badges worn by all members of Pioneer battalions. Bottom: Collar badges worn by all ranks of the 16th (City of Cardiff) Battalion, The Welsh Regiment, a Pals-type battalion raised in 1914 – bronze (left) and brass (right) specimens are illustrated.

Above: A selection of mostly brass (gilding-metal) shoulder-strap titles. Top row: Lincolnshire Regiment; Tyneside Irish; Devonshire Regiment. Second row: Leeds Pals; Sheffield City Battalion; Bradford Pals. Third row: 23rd Royal Fusiliers (1st Sportsman's); bimetal 1st Tyneside Scottish; Salford Pals. Fourth row: London Scottish; 4th Manchester Pals; Oldham Pals. Bottom row: 1st Birmingham City Battalion; The King's Own (with officer's lion collar badge); Royal Inniskilling Fusiliers.

THE BRITISH SOLDIER OF 1914–18

The cap badge forms part of a set of insignia intended to inform the observer, and to identify the wearer as a member of a particular regiment or corps. In 1914, those insignia were to be worn on the khaki uniform developed as a replacement for the traditional red coat of the British infantryman.

Other ranks' 1902 pattern serge Service Dress was intended for field conditions, in all weathers. Characteristically loose-fitting, the jacket had seven brass buttons of standard, General Service pattern. Patches at the shoulder bore the extra wear from the position of the rifle butt in action, and there were four ample external pockets with buttoned flaps. A simplified version was introduced in 1915 in an attempt to reduce manufacturing time, possessing none of the refinements of the original.

Other ranks' shoulder straps bore regimental insignia in the form of brass (gilding-metal) shoulder titles. A bewildering array was produced (though some regiments, the Guards in particular, used cloth titles). Many different types were produced for

Right: Brass (gilding-metal) proficiency badges, worn on the sleeve. From the top left: scout (appointment); marksman (skill-at-arms); bandsman (appointment); armourer (trade); gun-layer (appointment); machine-gunner (skill-at-arms); signaller (skill-at-arms), here showing the method of attachment to the sleeve.

Service battalions, which often simply wore the cap badge of the parent regiment. Collar badges were not generally used by other ranks until after the war but are to be seen in some units, particularly those serving as Pioneers.

Throughout the war, further insignia were added to the sleeves of the jacket, including rank badges, specialist proficiency badges, so-called 'battle patches' and divisional insignia. For other ranks, proficiency badges were intended to identify the specialist and are divisible into four types: trade or qualification badges (such as the crossed flags of the signaller); skill-at-arms, won during competition or in tests of ability (such as marksmen); appointments (such as bandsmen); and instructors. It was intended that these would be embroidered badges, but they are invariably seen as brass, attached through the sleeve by the addition of a back plate and cotter pin.

'Old sweats' – soldiers with long service – could be identified by a series of inverted chevrons on their lower left sleeve, one for every two years served with a clean record of service. Vertical stripes awarded for each incident of wounding would be worn beneath. From January 1918, smaller, coloured chevrons were worn on the lower sleeve of the right arm – one for each year of service overseas. In addition to these, by 1918 a bewildering array of colourful 'battle patches' and formation signs started to appear on the uniform, intended to identify division, brigade and even battalion for the onlooker.

Right: Soldier of the Duke of Wellington's Regiment, with machine-gunner (MG in wreath) and range-taker (R in wreath) brass skill-at-arms badges.

Far right: Lower left sleeve of a First World War period Service Dress jacket, with crossed-rifles marksman skill-at-arms badge; good conduct badge (inverted chevron) indicating two years' good conduct; and a wound badge, a single stripe indicating one incident of wounding.

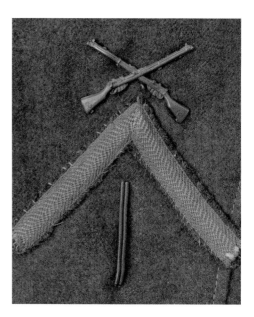

Officers' Service Dress, known as OSD, was to distinguish the rank of the wearer easily – so easily that it was to provide enemy snipers with a clear target to aim at. Tailored to the needs of the individual officer, each Service Dress jacket nevertheless had to conform to the standard sealed pattern. The collar bore 'facing' pairs of distinctive collar badges, usually bronzed; cap badges were also bronzed. Badges of rank were generally applied to the cuffs of the jacket, though. Some officers took it upon themselves to move these badges to the shoulder straps, an affectation that had always been used by the Guards.

Many Scottish regiments were kilted. Though warm to wear with its folds of woollen tartan, the kilt harboured lice and soaked up burdensome water; it was worn with a plain khaki 'apron' in the trenches. The Scottish Service Dress jacket was also special – its front skirts were cut back in the manner of a traditional doublet. To complement the appearance of the Highland soldier, there was a range of caps and bonnets; early in the war the commonest was the rakish glengarry, in a variety of patterns with various diced borders, coloured 'touries' (pompoms) and the flamboyant white-metal cap badge. Later the Scots adopted the khaki Tam o'Shanter,

Officers attending a musketry school. All wear equipment typical of their arms: leather bandoliers are worn by the cavalrymen (rear left); officers in infantry Service battalions wear 1914 pattern leather equipment (front right and rear centre); the rest wear 1908 pattern webbing, the standard load-bearing equipment of the infantryman. The officers present wear Officer's Service Dress; the sergeant instructor has crossed-rifles instructor's badges above his rank badges. A variety of cap badges are present. Rear row, left to right: Northamptonshire Yeomanry; Royal Scots Greys; Manchester Regiment; Essex Regiment; Lincolnshire Regiment (Lincolnshire officers had their own pattern badge); Durham Light Infantry. Front row, left to right: South Staffordshire Regiment; School of Musketry; Leeds Pals.

First World War period glengarry and white-metal badge of the 10th (Scottish) Battalion, The King's Liverpool Regiment TF.

a large, circular but otherwise shapeless object, with a range of tartan badge backings.

Khaki Drill, or 'KDs', was the standard uniform issued for warm climates and in appearance consisted of a cotton version of service dress. KDs were usually worn with the Wolseley pattern cork sun helmet, which provided protection only from the sun – protection enhanced by the use of additional neck flaps. A strip of cloth wound around it, known as the puggaree or pagri (terms for turban-like headgear derived from the British experience in India), would serve as the base for a badge of sorts.

In 1914 British soldiers – like all other combatants – went to war in headgear that was to provide an element of military smartness but one not designed to provide any kind of ballistic protection. For the average British soldier this was the peaked cap that had been adopted in 1905, with stiffened rim and peak. The cap badge, as commonly understood, was specifically designed to be carried on the front of all versions of this cap and was worn even in battle – though in some cases, such as in

Right: Soldier of a Service battalion of the Argyll and Sutherland Highlanders, wearing kilt, kilt apron and glengarry.

Far right: Soldier in Khaki Drill (KD) uniform and Wolseley pattern field service helmet. The cloth binding of the helmet, known as the puggaree, was often used for attaching badges.

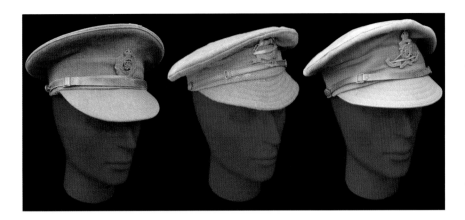

Service Dress caps. Left to right: post-war stiff Service Dress cap with George V period brass Royal Engineers badge – wartime caps have a narrower chin strap and smaller peak; 1916 pattern serge 'soft service dress cap' with West Yorkshire Regiment bimetal badge; 1918 pattern 'denim' (gabardine) cap with Royal Artillery brass badge.

trench raids, the badge could be blackened or discarded. In late 1914 the stiff cap was replaced by the floppy winter trench cap, known universally as the 'gor' blimy', in turn replaced in 1916–17 by the soft cap (in serge, and then 'denim' versions). Both were capable of being folded and stowed in the soldier's equipment, as they had no stiff components. Officers' caps, stiff at first, were also to become modified to a comfortable (and fashionable) softness by the war's end.

With head wounds common, there was a pressing need for increased head protection in the front line. The 'War Office pattern' helmet, patented by John Brodie, was introduced in late 1915. Pressed from non-magnetic steel, it had a sharp, unprotected rim, a dish-like form and a wide brim, and was intended to provide protection from above. An improved version appeared in response to criticism (the Mark 1), with an applied steel protective rim and sand finish. Cap badges appeared on both types. In many cases they consisted of a standard badge, its fittings removed, brazed to the front of the helmet. Regimental badges or formation signs were painted onto the shell of the helmet, or cloth badges were attached to the helmet covers that were fashioned from sacking.

So equipped, the British soldier would experience five long years of war – and would bring home his cap badge as a souvenir.

Steel 'Brodie' helmets with applied insignia. Left to right: Mark 1 with cover and applied insignia of the 9th (Scottish) Division; Mark 1 with painted 34th Division chequerboard divisional sign; Mark 1 with painted Notts and Derby regimental badge; War Office Pattern (Type B) with painted West Yorkshire regimental badge.

Chapter Two

THE CAP BADGE

THE CAP BADGE has been worn by the men of the British Army since 1897; yet its antecedents are much older, derived from feudal devices or liveries intended to identify a lord and distinguish his followers. In a military sense, distinguishing friend from foe on the battlefield was an important expedient, and the use of some identifying device in the years before uniforms was essential.

Though temporary 'field signs' (such as branches, foliage or paper scraps) had been used since at least the Middle Ages, perhaps the earliest metal military uniform badges were one-sided silver badges sewn directly onto their clothing by Royalist soldiers during the Civil War. With Cromwell's New Model Army in 1645 came an emphasis on uniformity, a principle that would continue with the Restoration of Charles II and beyond. The red-coated British infantryman derives from this time, his headdress mostly a simple, unornamented tricorn cap. Military headdress would change as civilian and military fashions developed. When the fashion for grenade-wielding grenadiers arrived from the Continent in 1678, the distinctive mitre-like grenadier cap was created, and with it the first formal insignia to be carried on headdress.

The Royal Warrant of 1751 is a turning point in the history of military uniforms. By Royal Decree of George II (the last British monarch to lead his army into battle), insignia carried on colours, guidons and grenadier caps was to conform to set patterns. No longer were the personal arms, crests or other devices of the regimental colonels to be carried upon the colours of the King's army; instead, only ancient devices, honours and mottoes sanctioned by the King could be allowed. From this point on, the elaborately fashioned grenadier cap – finished in the relevant facing colour of the regiment (blue for royal regiments) – would bear only the Latin motto *Nec aspera terrent* ('Nor hardship deter'), the white horse of Hanover and the regimental number on a turn-up at the rear of the cap. For those regiments honoured by their longevity and position, however, embroidered badges would be allowed, mirroring their prominent presence on the colours.

The wearing of metal headdress badges followed the introduction of the shako in 1800 – an unwieldy piece of broadly cylindrical (though often approaching bell-shaped) headgear that varied in form until it was abolished in 1878. Derived from Hungarian military fashion, the shako was worn by most infantrymen, fitted with a plate finished in brass. These plates varied in design as the helmet itself varied, and the prominent feature of most of them was the regimental number. The shako was replaced by a spiked cloth helmet (influenced by German military fashion), fitted with a numbered brass 'star' helmet plate. This helmet remained an item of full dress for infantry regiments other than Fusiliers (who wore sealskin caps with standard grenade badges) up to the First World War. With the dissolution of the numbered infantry regiments in 1881, a new helmet plate of universal pattern was produced.

Opposite:
Martial functionality.
The crossed machine guns
of the Machine Gun
Service (MGS) and
Motor Machine Gun
Service (MMGS) leave
nothing to the
imagination.

Right: Illustrations of British soldiers from the 'Clotheing Book' of 1742. Left: A soldier of a royal regiment, the Royal North British Fusiliers ('Royal Scotch Fusiliers'), with blue facings and mitre cap. Right: An infantryman of the 37th Regiment of Foot (North Hampshire), with unadorned tricorn hat and yellow facings.

Royal Scotch Fuziliers.   37ᵗ⁴ Regiment of Foot.

Below: Reproduction of a c. 1829–39 shako, with simple star shako plate for the 24th Regiment of Foot (2nd Warwickshire). This regiment would later find fame at Rorke's Drift in 1879.

This had a removable centre with a regimental badge, most usually surrounded by a circlet with the regimental title. The helmet plate centre would be valuable as a separate badge in its own right, useful particularly when the glengarry was introduced in 1874 for all ranks in 'undress' – that is, when not in full ceremonial uniform.

With the arrival of khaki Service Dress came the adoption of a cap. At first, this was the peakless 'Brodrick' cap, an unsuccessful and short-lived experiment quickly replaced by the peaked Service Dress cap. New badges

*Left:
Helmet plate centre (HPC) from the universal helmet plate (1881–1914) for The Duke of Cambridge's Own (Middlesex Regiment).*

"MY daddy's a soldier now!"

Above left: Universal helmet plates from the blue cloth helmet, introduced in 1878. Left: Pre-1881 plate for the 97th Foot. Right: Post-1881 (pre-1902) plate for The Border Regiment.

Above: Wartime sentimental postcard, depicting in detail the standard 1905 pattern Service Dress cap, with attached white-metal cap badge of the 9th Lancers. Depictions of cap badges in this way were very popular during the war.

Left: Typical crowns encountered on cap badges, here on examples from the Army Service Corps and its post-war successor, the Royal Army Service Corps. Top: Queen Victoria's crown on ASC badge; Tudor (Imperial or King's) crown on George V vintage ASC badge. Bottom: Tudor crown (and GRVI cypher) on Second World War vintage RASC badge; St Edward's (or Queen Elizabeth II) crown on post-1953 vintage RASC badge.

Above: Cap badges associated with Light Infantry (bugles) and Fusilier (flaming grenade) roles. Top: Oxfordshire and Buckinghamshire Light Infantry, Duke of Cornwall's Light Infantry. Bottom: Royal Inniskilling Fusiliers, Northumberland Fusiliers.

Above right: Battle honour devices on cap badges. Top: Dorsetshire Regiment, Essex Regiment, both bearing the castle and key of Gibraltar, awarded for the defence of the Rock in 1779–83. Bottom: Gloucestershire Regiment, Lincolnshire Regiment, bearing the sphinx, commemorating action against the French in Egypt during 1801.

were called for, as both cap types were provided with bands that were too small to accept the helmet plate centre. From 1898, new cap badge designs were in place that, in most cases, would vary only slightly (with a change in crown from that of Victoria to the Tudor or Imperial crown worn by the kings) over the first half of the twentieth century. These badges would come to represent the regiment, being widely used and reproduced in a number of settings, domestic and military.

The typical cap badge is composed of several components. First is the identification of trade or function, usually associated with hardware or weaponry, commonly seen in the support arms and services. Typical are the machine gun, artillery piece and tank of the Machine Gun Corps, Royal Regiment of Artillery and Tank Corps respectively. These devices leave little to the imagination; others rely upon heraldic or mythological aspects, such as the rod of Aesculapius, the traditional symbol of medicine, borne by the Royal Army Medical Corps. For the fighting arms, function may be a little more obscure, though cavalry regiments often display the tools of their trade. For Light Infantry, the bugle is commonly seen, as the bugle was used in place of the cumbersome drum for signalling orders in action for light troops. The flaming grenade of Fusilier regiments is another historical artefact, Fusiliers serving originally as protection for artillery units.

The second component typical of cap badges is the bearing of an ancient badge or device, and many date back centuries. Named in the 1751 warrant that regulated regimental insignia were 'the Royal regiments and six old corps' – fourteen regiments that were permitted to carry forward badges and devices that had been associated with them since their formation, and that had been carried on their colours, emphasising the direct link between badge and colour. The origin of some of these, such as the acorn of the 22nd Foot (Cheshire Regiment), is obscure. Royal devices, such as the Prince of Wales's plume of feathers, ducal coronets and crowns, and elements of the orders of chivalry are also common cap badge components, and all of them attest to historic royal links.

Battle honours are a third, significant part of the structure of the common cap badge. The most evident are devices granted for actions: these include the castle and key of Gibraltar, awarded for action during the siege of Gibraltar in 1779–83, and the sphinx, granted for action against the French in Egypt during 1801. In other cases, single or multiple honours are displayed, awarded for battles in which the regiment played a major part. Battle honours are inscribed upon regimental colours; for Rifle regiments, units lacking military banners in their light roles, the inscription of honours on cap badges has a greater significance. The award of honours was initially by royal sanction; however, as more and more regiments and their battalions took part in the 'small wars' of the Victorian era, thereby claiming new honours, some regulation was deemed necessary.

Cap badges of two of the Irish regiments disbanded upon the formation of the Irish Free State in 1922: The Royal Irish Regiment and The Royal Dublin Fusiliers.

Following the Second Boer War, a commission was set up to examine the parameters of battle honour qualification. To qualify for honours, at least 50 per cent of a battalion, together with its headquarters, had to be present at an engagement – rules that would still be in place following the First World War. This meant that Volunteer battalions and their successors the Territorials, though often wearing a cap badge identical to that of their parent regiment, had to strike out honours granted to their Regulars, though most, having served in the Second Boer War of 1899–1902, had at least one of their own.

Finally, mottoes are common and distinctive cap badge components. Most are derived from historic feudal connections; many others represent 'mission statements', in current parlance. A good command of Latin helps in their interpretation – though mottoes appear in many other languages, German and French among them.

Following the First World War, many regiments and corps were to receive changes in title, being awarded the honour of being 'Royal'. Many others would disappear or suffer amalgamations, which have continued to the present day. In 1922, when Ireland re-emerged as an independent nation, the five Irish infantry regiments in the British Army (The Royal Irish Regiment, Connaught Rangers, Leinsters, Munster Fusiliers and Dublin Fusiliers) were disbanded, and southern Irish cavalry regiments merged with English counterparts. Other changes would be made in the inter-war years: a new arm – the Royal Signals – and new services would be created; the Cyclists concept would be abandoned; the London Regiment was broken up; the Cavalry and Yeomanry were down-sized, their regiments merged; and, finally, some Territorial infantry battalions would be redeployed to the support arms of Artillery, Engineers or Signals. All of these changes would materially affect the cap badges worn. New infantry badge designs would appear, and Territorials would be granted the right to share in the battle honours of the Regulars, their distinctive badges being no longer worn (though, excepting the London Regiment, the four Territorial infantry regiments would continue). These changes are such that some badges differ materially from their Great War counterparts.

Pragmatically, the use of regimental insignia on caps and other headdress was intended to identify the unit to the casual observer, but there is more to it than that.

Propagation of the 'love of one's regiment' was a very real principle in cementing the solid relationship between a soldier and his unit. One of the purposes of the Caldwell-Childers reforms was the creation of what would be called today a 'sustainable future' for the regiments. By anchoring them to a specific county, it was expected that local men would feel kinship with their local units. Whereas the ancient British Army depended on life-serving 'old sweats', the new reforms, with their limited service periods, were intended to deliver a younger army. This was heavily dependent upon active recruiting, and the lure of the ancient symbols embodied in the cap badge was one of the ways that the heroic and historic actions of the recruits' forebears could be appropriated for their own use. Recruits to a regiment were (and are to this day) taught to respect its traditions and honours won through its centuries of campaigning. Cap badges represent in miniature a compressed time capsule of the achievements of the regiment, but they mean much more. *Esprit de corps* – difficult to measure but deemed essential in a well-trained force as a linchpin of morale – was therefore, at least partially, to be maintained through pride in a cap badge, and the wearing of it.

Badges and Their Meaning: *a wartime (c. 1917) publication, one of several on similar subjects published by George Philip & Son in order to assist the observer in interpreting the increasingly bewildering array of military badges.*

It is not surprising, therefore, that the most potent and portable symbol of the regiment – the cap badge – was sought after by schoolboy collectors and treasured by the soldiers themselves. Often soldiers compiled their own collections of badges of fellow corps and wore them as trophies attached to belts, a kind of folk art. Cap badges are also common themes of craft outputs that created souvenirs intended for the fighting man. Typical would be 'trench art' souvenirs made from scrap munitions at the front (or, more likely, made behind the lines and sold to the returning fighting men), souvenirs that would feature buttons and cap badges brazed to the metal of spent shell cases. In other cases these would be specially commissioned and beautifully crafted, carrying the initials of the maker or bearer – with many more produced post-war.

Highly prized wartime crafts are the silk postcards produced close to the battlefront by women working in a cottage industry, their nimble fingers turning out hand-embroidered designs. Regimental badges, with all their intricate details, were often faithfully reproduced in silk thread, sent

home as representations of the service of a loved one at the front. Embroidery and needlework figuring cap badges would also be created by wives and sweethearts at home; typical are the heart-shaped cushions much in vogue at the time, the central device being a representation of the regimental badge of the soldier.

The appropriation of the cap badge as a tangible representation of the emotional bond between a soldier and his loved one has perhaps no better example than 'sweetheart' jewellery. Such jewels, typically brooches, commonly have as a centrepiece the faithful representation of a military badge in miniature, often enamelled, and in some cases finished in precious metals. Though some of these – known as 'mufti badges' – were to distinguish the soldier out of uniform (and in the case of the Pals

Top left: Wartime collection of Leeds Pals' badges and insignia assembled by Second Lieutenant Tom Willey of the 15th (Service) Battalion, Prince of Wales's Own (West Yorkshire Regiment) (1st Leeds). Lieutenant Willey was killed on the first day of the Battle of the Somme, 1 July 1916.

Top right: Trench art often includes regimental insignia, here a 1916 all-brass economy issue badge of the Royal Sussex Regiment, attached to a piece of shell brass to form a match fold.

Left: A wartime family group: father, a private in the Royal Fusiliers; son, proudly wearing a cap badge of the Royal Artillery and clutching a piece of trench art made from shell brass; mother, wearing the armlet of the Women's Land Army.

Above: 'Sweetheart' brooches – miniature depictions of military badges – usually given by soldiers to their wives and sweethearts as a forget-me-not. Top: Tyneside Scottish, Machine Gun Corps. Centre: Liverpool pals. Bottom: Cardiff City Battalion, Welsh Regiment; Liverpool Pals.

Above right: Silk postcards, made by women in northern France and sold to soldiers. Highly prized – then and now – are those that depict military badges.

Above: A cushion with beadwork picking out the regimental badge of the Royal Sussex Regiment. Such mementoes were often hand-made by women in honour of the military service of their men.

phenomenon, representing the only 'uniform' issued), for most their purpose was as a gift and a forget-me-not, the recipient wearing the badge in remembrance of their soldier on active service. In other cases, the cap badge itself would be given to children or loved ones, sometimes modified for easy wearing on civilian dress, at other times on uniform worn fleetingly and coyly by women at home for the photographer.

The Fovant Badges – military badges cut into the chalk downland adjacent to the Wiltshire village of Fovant – are reminders today of the thousands of men from many military units who trained here during the First World War. Drawing deeply on the tradition of the white horse – centuries-old depictions of horses and other figures cut through the turf to the white chalk below – the Fovant Badges were produced by the men both as light relief from their other responsibilities, and also from pride in their regiments. Surviving today through the efforts of dedicated volunteer conservationists, the Fovant Badges typify the way in which the recruit readily 'bought into' the regimental ethos expressed by the badge itself. In a smaller, more personal way, soldiers on active service, in billets, or even at the front line, would create their own badges through the simple act of the creation of graffiti. Such regimental graffiti are commonly encountered in the chalk tunnels of Picardy, and especially in the city of Arras, undermined by many tunnels that led to the front line in April 1917.

Perhaps the most poignant of all representations of the military cap badge is that of their faithful depiction on the elegant Portland stone headstones that mark the graves of the men (and women) who fell in the two world wars. The decision to replace the original wooden crosses with something more permanent was taken in 1917–18, before the war had ended, following recommendations made to the Imperial War Graves Commission by Lieutenant-Colonel Sir Frederic Kenyon, Director of the British Museum:

Four women pose for the camera in the uniforms normally worn by their menfolk, with The Cambridgeshire Regiment, The Queen's Regiment and The 8th (Royal Irish) Hussars, and an unidentified regiment represented.

> In order to secure a certain amount of variety in uniformity and at the same time to gratify the regimental feeling which is so strong a characteristic of the British Army, it is proposed that each regiment … should have its own pattern of headstone, incorporating the regimental badge, which will be erected over the grave of every man of that regiment, wherever he may be buried, and will strike the note of dignity and solemnity, accompanied by the spirit of hopefulness and pride proper to the resting places of those who have died with glory and not in vain.

Above: The Fovant Badges. Aerial view of the regimental badges carved by soldiers through the turf to reveal the white chalk beneath, and restored by the Fovant Badges Society. From left to right the badges are: Royal Wiltshire Yeomanry (added following the Second World War); 6th London Regiment (City of London Rifles) (cut in 1916); Australian Commonwealth Military Forces (worn by most of the Australian Imperial Forces, and cut by them in 1916–17); Royal Corps of Signals (added in 1970); The Wiltshire Regiment (post-Second World War); 5th London Regiment (London Rifle Brigade) (cut in 1916); 8th London Regiment (Post Office Rifles) (added in 1916); Devonshire Regiment (cut in 1916).

Below: Commonwealth War Graves Commission headstones in Ypres Reservoir Cemetery, Belgium, two of them marking unknown soldiers – their regiments identified by regimental badges.

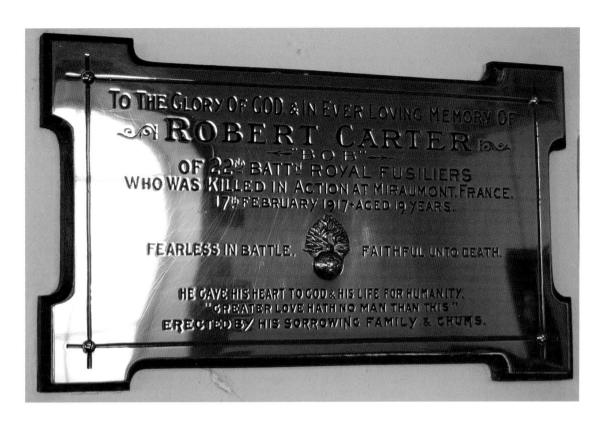

These headstones continue to serve their purpose today. Many of the gravestones encountered in the cemeteries of the Western Front mark graves that cannot be attributed to a known individual; yet, for these men, fellowship with their regiment is maintained by the presence of the regimental inscription on their headstones – derived from the cap badge found with the soldier on the battlefield. This principle continues as further remains of the missing are released from the soil of Flanders today. Personal memorials, cards and other *memento mori* announcing the death of a soldier take the same tack: in death, the love of the regiment reflected back, through the use of the regimental symbol, on the man who gave his life.

All regiments had suffered in the First World War and would fight again in the Second; the men of Rifle regiments, whose traditions dictated that honours be carried on the badges themselves, would go to battle with remembrance of the First World War on their caps – the 1st Monmouthshire Regiment bearing its honours on a wreath of Flanders poppies, a fitting remembrance of lost comrades.

Top:
Brass memorial plaque in Low Bentham Methodist Church, Lancashire, to Private Robert Carter of the 22nd (Service) Battalion, Royal Fusiliers (Kensington), who was killed in action on the Somme, February 1917.

Right:
Post-war cap badge of the 1st Battalion, Monmouthshire Regiment, incorporating Flanders poppies and First World War battle honours.

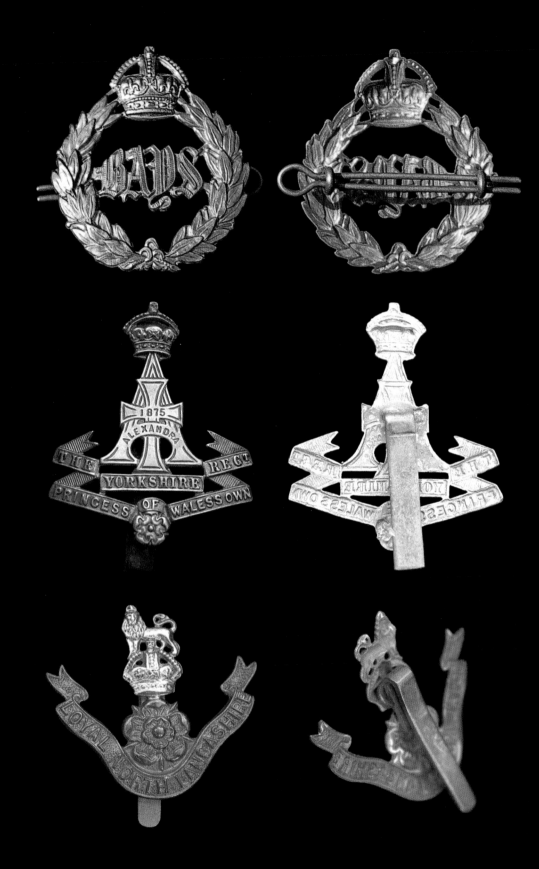

Chapter Three

CAP BADGE CONSTRUCTION

URING THE First World War cap badges were usually made from copper-alloy metal, though some, such as the early devices of 'Kitchener's Army', can be found in a diversity of materials, from paper labels to enamelled badges. The commonest material used for cap badges is one of the family of copper–zinc alloys known collectively as brass. Brass is a highly variable alloy with at least 50 per cent copper, the proportion of copper to zinc determining the physical properties of the material. Brass is used widely for decorative purposes but also has many important applications in munitions. 'Yellow brass', an alloy of 67 per cent copper and 33 per cent zinc, was used widely for military badges until the 1890s, when it was replaced by 'gilding metal'. Gilding metal is a brass alloy with a much higher copper content, around 87 per cent, with a correspondingly lower zinc component, and is so called because of its suitability for gilding. With its higher copper content, gilding metal has a pleasing dark golden colour, less harsh than yellow brass. Given its copper content, it is not surprising that gilding metal is the softest of the brass family, used in ammunition components, such as the drive bands of shells, and shell cases. Some purists insist on the use of the term 'gilding metal' in describing badges, but it is just as correct to call it 'brass'. This tack is taken here.

Whereas brass is the most common metal used in cap badges, associated with it is what was once termed 'German silver', a silver-coloured copper–zinc–nickel alloy. It is the use of nickel in the mix that creates the silver colour; without it, this metal would simply be one of the brass family. The term 'German silver' was largely replaced by the widely used but non-specific 'white metal', a name also used for a wide range of brittle metal alloys. White metal as used in cap badges is an alloy of copper (64.5 per cent), zinc (16.5 per cent) and nickel (19 per cent). Like brass, it is suitable for cap badge construction, in that it takes a high shine and produces a crisp badge when die-struck during the manufacturing process.

Brass and white metal are also commonly combined to create 'bimetal' badges. Usually, bimetal badges have a body of one metal (brass or white metal), with features in a different alloy added to them. A distinctive characteristic of badges in which one metal is applied directly to the face of another is the presence of holes in the foundation metal, beneath the additional feature. Known to collectors as 'braze' or 'sweat' holes, these are thought to have been essential to the manufacturing process, perhaps containing the flux used in brazing, or allowing the escape of gases. The presence of braze holes is widely held to be a reliable indicator of a period badge; some genuine examples, however, do lack braze holes. In other cases additional scrolls are attached beneath the badge by tabs brazed directly to its lower part.

Opposite:
Badge fitments. Top:
Queen's Bays – loops
and cotter pin. Centre:
Yorkshire Regiment –
vertical shank, or slider.
This has the crimp mark
and has been cut short to
improve fit. Bottom: Loyal
Regiment – 'hairpin'
slider, its top folded over
to provide further support
for the design.

Above: Typical metals used in cap-badge construction. Top: The Buffs, in brass (gilding metal); The Border Regiment, in white metal (with red cloth insert). Bottom: The Cheshire Regiment, bimetal (left) and all-brass economy strike (right).

Above right: Army Service Corps officer's cap badge (or large-pattern collar badge) in bronze, manufactured by Jennens & Company (J & Co). Loops are the fitment here; folding 'blades' are more common.

Other metals are used in addition to brass and white metal; bronze is typical of officers' badges, purchased from military outfitters, their uniforms being made by specialist tailors. Bronze is also encountered on some other ranks' badges, too. Silver is another metal commonly seen in officers' badges, often used in conjunction with gilt and even enamel, but these materials were not meant to be used with Service Dress intended for front-line use and are mostly used post-war. Hallmarked silver can also be seen in some presentation badges, like those given to the first volunteers of the Liverpool Pals and the Lonsdale Battalion in 1914.

The manufacture of cap badges usually conforms to one of three main types: die-struck, die-cast or sand-cast. Die-striking, the commonest method, involves sheets of metal struck between opposing male and female dies, thereby forming the badge. Voids (holes) would then be cut as part of the design, and the badge trimmed. Die-struck badges have a representation of the device on the front, as well as the reverse of the badge. In contrast, die-casting involves the forcing of molten metal into a mould of two halves (the halves known also as dies), and usually such badges have a clear representation of the badge device only at the front. Sand-cast badges are sometimes seen in regiments that served overseas in Africa and Asia, and were locally bought and obtained as replacements of the standard pattern. The method requires a pattern – usually an existing badge – to be forced into a sand mixture to act as the mould, into which is forced molten metal. Some collectors consider these badges suspect, but they may be as much part of the history of the regiment as the standard type.

The multi-stage manufacturing process used to create bimetal cap badges was time-consuming, so from 1916 to the end of the war many bimetal badges were produced in brass alone, known collectively as 'economy strikes'. In the same way, badges that required cut-outs, known as 'voids', were produced as solid badges. Use of brass avoided the use of nickel, a metal in demand for munitions, and this explains why many white-metal badges were also produced in brass, again an economy measure employed from 1916.

The fitments used on cap badges vary. Up to 1903 badges were usually fixed to the cap using loops (also known as 'shanks' or 'lugs'), most commonly fashioned out of copper wire and attached to the back of the badge during manufacturing.

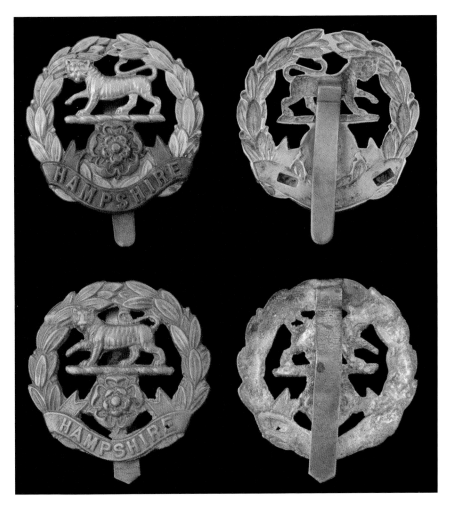

Left: Differing cap-badge construction methods demonstrated by Hampshire Regiment examples. Top: Die-struck, bimetal badge. The rear of the badge shows typical 'sweat' or 'braze' holes indicating the attachment of brass features to a white-metal badge. The slider has the crimp mark. Bottom: Locally made, brass sand-cast version based on the bimetal version. Some of these were made in theatre; others are post-war.

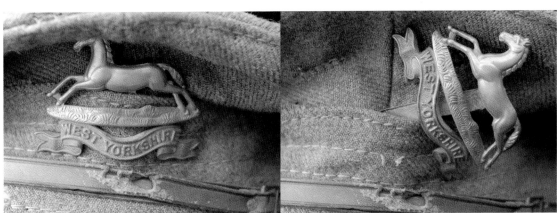

Above:
A well-worn 1916 pattern soft cap showing the fitment of a badge with slider, that of the Prince of Wales's Own (West Yorkshire) Regiment.

Top:
Srengthening applied, according to regulation, to the rear of a wartime Royal Artillery cap badge. Similar strengthening was applied to badges with weaker design elements, such as that of the Connaught Rangers.

Bottom left:
Cap badges marked with the regimental number of the owner. Top: Period-repaired slider of a soldier of the 2nd Life Guards. Bottom: Badge belonging to Private Albert Phillips of the East Yorkshire Regiment, who survived the war, having first landed in France in February 1915.

Bottom right:
Makers' marks, sometimes encountered on badges. Top: 'Lambourne & Co Birmingham', stamped on the slider of a Territorial cap badge of the Suffolk Regiment. Centre: 'J.R. Gaunt London' plaque fitted to the rear of a Hood Battalion, RND, badge. Bottom: 'B P & Co. Ltd. B'ham' (Bent, Parker & Company), stamped on the slider of an East Lancashire Regiment badge.

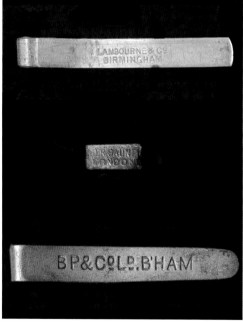

These passed through holes in the cap and were kept in place by a 'cotter pin', a loop of wire bent to create tension. Loops are less common on badges of the First World War period, but are typical of the white-metal badges of the Scottish regiments, the brass badges of the Guards and the Royal Naval Division, and a variety of other badge types.

A much more common fitment used during the First World War was the 'slider' (officially known as a 'vertical shank') – a narrow strip of brass (or, much more rarely, white metal) attached to the rear of the badge and bent to provide space between the rear of the badge and the slider itself. This allowed the fitting to be 'slid' behind the band of the Service Dress cap. Original sliders vary in form but usually have a distinctive 'crimp' mark, produced presumably as part of the bending process. Some are bent to form additional support to the rear of the badge (known as 'hairpin sliders' to collectors). Early-pattern sliders were long; it is common to find them cut down, presumably to stop them impacting the head of the wearer, when fitted. Well-used badges may have their sliders replaced or repaired; this is part of the functional life of the badge. In other cases, additional strengthening is applied to the rear of those badges with delicate features.

Sliders are sometimes stamped with the name of the manufacturer or, rarely, with the regimental number of the owner. Some makers' marks are reliable indicators of a genuine badge; this is particularly true of the small 'J.R. Gaunt London' plaque attached to the rear of the Royal Naval Division badges, and the brass issue of the 11th Battalion (Lonsdale). Conversely, the mark 'J.R.Gaunt.London', measuring 15 mm in length, is universally considered to be the mark of badges reproduced in the 1970s. In rare examples, stout brooch-type pins are used as a primary fixing device, most commonly in some Scottish headdress badges. More commonly, badges have been secondarily 'brooched' to serve as a 'sweetheart' badge, or to be worn by

Top left:
Use of similar design features. Several of the London Regiment Territorial battalions (such as the 6th Battalion, right) employ the Maltese cross originally used by the King's Royal Rifle Corps (left).

Top right:
Period 'brooching' of a cap badge, in this case an example from the Royal Engineers. Brooching involves removal of the original fitments and the addition of a pin for use as a 'sweetheart' or 'mufti' badge. This one belonged to Sapper J. Briggs, veteran of the Guards Division, 1915–18.

Reproduction 5th London Regiment (London Rifle Brigade) cap badge. The badge is thin, has low relief, is not well struck and has the tell-tale 'J.R.Gaunt. London' ('Gaunt with a dot') 15 mm mark on its slider that is associated with badges reproduced in the 1970s.

honourably discharged soldiers as a souvenir of service. Of all things, the act of 'brooching' perhaps highlights the very real emotional bond felt by the soldier for his regiment.

Cap badges provide the historian with a valuable means of identifying, at least in part, the regiment or battalion of an individual. In many cases, this involves scrutiny of photographs, and the comparison with specimens in collections, military museums and reference works. Many badges are confusing, however, with some conforming to the same basic pattern – this is particularly true of the Maltese cross pattern used by the King's Royal Rifle Corps, and by at least three or four Territorial battalions of other regiments. As such, there is no substitute for having the badge actually in your hand to study. While the identification of soldiers may be of the greatest significance to historians and families alike, cap badges have attracted interest from generations of collectors, including the soldiers themselves.

Highly portable and relatively inexpensive objects, cap badges have been collected avidly almost from the inception of separate military insignia on uniforms. Yet, as with all areas of collecting, amassing collections of military badges is fraught with difficulty. Experience and 'feel' are the only true defence against the host of fakers and forgers who are out to separate collectors from their cash, and this is particularly true in the age of internet auctions. In most cases, value is arbitrary but in terms of relative cost one could put the badges described in this book into the following ascending order: standard arms and services; standard infantry badges; Cavalry; Yeomanry; Territorial battalions; Service (Pals') battalions.

Reproduction Pals' badges. Original badges of 'Kitchener's Army' are much sought after and are often reproduced. Top: 1st Birmingham Battalion, Royal Warwickshire Regiment ('Birmingham Pals'). The badge is of low relief, differs in design (lacking hair on the pelt of the antelope, among other features) and has the tell-tale stamp 'J. R. Gaunt. London'. Despite this, the badge has been chemically 'aged' to deceive. Bottom: 1st and 2nd Leeds Battalions, West Yorkshire Regiment ('Leeds Pals'). In low relief, the design differs in detail – 'skinny' owls with long legs, and pronounced 'dots' on the shield top. Here, metal polish residue has been lightly applied to the rear of the badge to give a sense of age.

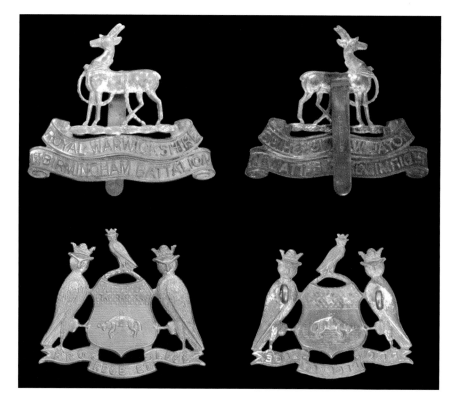

Fakes and forgeries – and so-called 'restrikes' – are common now, and their prevalence is off-putting, particularly with rarer specimens. If a short-lived First World War Service battalion comprised a thousand men, with replacements of perhaps another thousand men during its existence, then it stands to reason that such badges might be rarer than one would be led to believe by their constant re-occurrence on internet auction sites; *caveat emptor*. As such, seeking out a real rarity can be a trying experience. It is common for fake cap badges to be chemically aged, with the application of materials that are intended to give the impression of years of accumulated metal polish. Badges caked in this material are often suspect.

Technically, 'restrikes' are badges that have been made using the original dies and are therefore arguably closer to the original. Among the first badges to be created in this way were reproductions of the Victorian glengarry badges specially struck for collectors in the early twentieth century. In the 1970s many original wartime cap badges were reproduced, and that trend has continued unabated to the present day. Though some were conceivably 'restruck', in many cases reproductions were created from new dies that were modelled on the original. These will have subtle, but distinct, differences in design. Whereas there could be some claim for originality with 'restruck' badges, there can surely be no similar claims made for reproductions. There are also 'fantasy' pieces – unrecorded badges satisfying the desire for the unusual badge. One such example is that created for the 17th and 23rd (1st and 2nd Football) Battalions of the Middlesex Regiment, even though the standard Middlesex badge was worn. This well-made fantasy creation has an applied football and corner flags; its authenticity continues to be debated.

In the chapters that follow, we have tried wherever possible to source and illustrate genuine examples of the main cap badges worn during the First World War. The majority of badges – infantry, cavalry and services – have dimensions that fall within a range of 40–45 mm high by 40–45 mm wide. Designed for the glengarry, Scots badges (and some others, such as that of the City of London Yeomanry) are larger, displaying a range of sizes from 50 to 75 mm high and 50 to 60 mm wide; large showy pieces, these contrast with less common smaller badges, such as those of the King's Own Yorkshire Light Infantry, the 13th Hussars or the 19th Lancers, tiny at around 30–33 mm high and 15–20 mm wide.

Most commonly encountered by the collector, only other ranks' badges are described here; most examples worn by officers with Service Dress during the war were bronzed, generally better-quality versions of the other ranks' badges. However, there are variants belonging to special patterns worn by officers alone, though many of these were post-war. Examples of these are illustrated by Arthur Kipling and Hugh King (*Headdress Badges of the British Army*) and by Major T. J. Edwards (*Regimental Badges*). Regimental titles employed here are as given in Brigadier E. A. James's book *British Regiments 1914–18*.

Probable 'fantasy' badge created to fulfil a desire for unusual pieces. This well-made badge is supposed to have been made for the 1st and 2nd Football Battalions of the Middlesex Regiment, despite there being no contemporary records of its issue. Nevertheless, the authenticity of this badge continues to be debated.

Chapter Four

CAP BADGES OF THE CAVALRY

T HE MOST SENIOR and, in past times, most flamboyant regiments of the British Army, ranked in order of precedence in front of the Infantry, are those of the Cavalry. Divided traditionally into Household Cavalry, intended to defend the monarch, and Cavalry of the Line, so called because of its historical formations in the line of battle, the Cavalry was to see action in the First World War, both in its intended role and as dismounted infantry. Lancers would see action with their preferred weapon early in the war, and others the traditional *arme blanche;* most, however, would use the Lee Enfield in the trenches. After the war, the cavalry would be reorganised, and ultimately mechanised, to meet a new threat.

Three cavalrymen 'somewhere in France'. Left to right: 18th Hussars, 2nd Life Guards, Queen's Bays. The two men on the right are qualified signallers. All wear spurs.

THE HOUSEHOLD CAVALRY

The Life Guards

The simple brass cap badges of the two regiments of Life Guards (1st and 2nd, distinguished by regimental title) reflect their origins in 1660 as four troops of horse charged with the protection of the monarch, with the royal cypher central to the design.

The Royal Horse Guards

The Royal Horse Guards were placed on equal footing with the regiments of the Household Cavalry as late as 1827 but had been raised in 1661 by the Earl of Oxford (hence their nickname, the 'Oxford Blues', later shortened to 'The Blues'). Serving in the same capacity as the Life Guards, they wore essentially the same brass cap badge – but with the title 'Royal Horse Guards'.

The Household Battalion

Not strictly a Cavalry unit, this battalion was raised in 1916 from reservists of the Household Cavalry. It was to serve on the Western Front in an infantry role and wore the badge illustrated, in brass or bronze.

CAVALRY OF THE LINE

The 1st (King's) Dragoon Guards

Emperor Franz Joseph I of Austria-Hungary was the Colonel of this regiment from 1896 to 1914 (his tenure ceasing with the outbreak of war), and the regiment wore his personal arms as a brass badge, until anti-Austrian feeling saw it replaced with the bimetal star badge in 1915 (an all-brass economy strike was issued in 1916).

Soldier of the Second Dragoon Guards (Queen's Bays).

The 2nd Dragoon Guards (Queen's Bays)

The badge of the Queen's Bays relates to their nickname – derived from the practice early on for its members to be mounted on bay-coloured horses. The name was accepted officially in 1870 and used as part of the all-brass cap badge from the later nineteenth century. The badge illustrated has loop fitments; sliders were more common during the war.

The 3rd (Prince of Wales's) Dragoon Guards

In common with many regiments associated with the Prince of Wales, the 3rd Dragoon Guards used white-metal plumes, and motto (*Ich dien* – 'I serve') granted as an honour to the regiment in 1765, with brass coronet and title. An all-brass economy strike appeared in 1916.

The 4th (Royal Irish) Dragoon Guards

The Royal Irish Dragoon Guards were distinguished by the star of the Order of St Patrick, founded by George III in 1783, the regiment taking its title as 'Royal Irish' in 1788. The badge is bimetal, the star in white metal, the title in brass. The 4th Dragoon Guards were first to engage the Germans in 1914.

The 5th (Princess Charlotte of Wales's) Dragoon Guards

The badge of the 5th Dragoon Guards was simple: the white horse of Hanover and the regimental title 'VDG' on a white metal centre, surrounded by a brass circle with the motto *Vestigia nulla retrorsum* – 'No turning back'. An all-brass version was struck in 1916.

The 6th Dragoon Guards (Carabiniers)

The Carabiniers' badge is distinguished by the tools of their trade – crossed carbines in brass. The central abbreviated title 'VIDG' is in white metal, surrounded by the motto of the Garter, in brass. The regiment gained its title in 1788, a fashionable term associated with long horse pistols that was given to a variety of regiments across Europe. An all-brass version of this badge was issued in 1916.

The 7th (Princess Royal's) Dragoon Guards

In 1720 this regiment was styled 'Ligonier's Horse' after its long-term Colonel, Earl Ligonier. Though the Royal Warrant of 1751 deleted the devices of regimental colonels from colours and guidons, his crest (a lion rampant issuing from a coronet) was to reappear, over his motto *Quo fata vocant* ('Wherever fate calls'), as the cap badge of this regiment in 1898, at first in white metal, then, from 1906, all in brass.

The 1st (Royal) Dragoons

The Royals are an ancient cavalry regiment, dating back to 1661, and bearing the battle honour 'Tangier, 1662–80'. At Waterloo the regiment distinguished itself by capturing the French 105th Regiment's eagle, a device granted to the regiment in 1838. Although brass eagle cap badges were made privately, the official insignia was based on the brass royal crest (crown and lion), with white-metal title scroll. The Kaiser was Colonel-in-Chief from 1894 – a situation that soon became vacant at the outbreak of war, to be filled by King George V.

The 2nd Dragoons (Royal Scots Greys)

The Royal Scots Greys had a distinguished record in battle, particularly against the French at Ramillies in 1706, and again at Waterloo in 1815. Their distinctive bimetal badge, with white metal eagle and the title 'Waterloo', commemorates the achievement of the capture of the eagle and flag of the French 45th Regiment during this famous battle.

The 3rd (King's Own) Hussars

The white horse of Hanover was granted to the regiment in 1768 (with the motto *Nec aspera terrent,* 'nor hardship deter'), but its title 'The King's Own' dates back even further, to George I in 1714. The bimetal cap badge of this regiment reflects these two elements, yet is easily confused with that of the West Yorkshire Regiment, which has similar design elements.

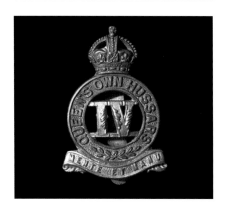

The 4th (Queen's Own) Hussars

The badge of this regiment centres on the prominent white-metal Roman numeral 'IV' within a crowned brass band carrying the regimental title. The white-metal motto scroll *Mente et manu* ('With heart and hand') was added to the badge in 1906. Several minor variants are known.

The 5th (Royal Irish) Lancers

The first of several badges bearing tools of the Lancers' trade – crossed lances – this badge bears the motto *Quis separabit* ('Who shall separate us?') of the Order of St Patrick, usually associated with Irish regiments. The lances have pennons of brass over white metal – reflecting the red and white pennons (derived from the Polish flag) of the real thing. There is an all-brass version of this badge, issued in 1916. In 1922 this regiment, based in Dublin, would merge with the 16th Lancers.

The 6th (Inniskilling) Dragoons

This regiment, together with the Royal Inniskilling Fusiliers, formed part of William III's defence of the castle of Inniskilling in northern Ireland against the forces of the deposed James II in 1688. The castle would figure in the insignia of both regiments, flying St George's flag. Many reproductions exist of this bimetal badge; they are distinguished by fewer brick courses on the central tower, and castle windows that are not voided. An all-brass economy strike was issued in 1916. This regiment remained in the British Army after 1922.

The 7th (Queen's Own) Hussars

The Queen's Own Hussars wore the simple badge illustrated, brass with the fancy white-metal monogram 'QO' applied to its centre. There is also an all-brass version, produced in 1916. The royal title refers to Caroline of Ansbach, consort of King George II, the regiment having received royal favour while she was still Princess of Wales, in 1715.

The 8th (King's Royal Irish) Hussars

This badge resembles that of at least two other units: the 8th (Irish) Battalion King's Liverpool Regiment, and the North Irish Horse, a Yeomanry regiment. In common with these and other corps with Irish connections, the 8th Hussars wore the bimetal 'angel' harp badge – though an all-brass version was issued in 1916. Reputedly raised from Protestant veterans of the Battle of the Boyne in 1690, the regiment survived in the British Army following the formation of the Irish Free State in 1922.

The 9th (Queen's Royal) Lancers

In common with most Lancer regiments, this one displays the tools of its trade, the crossed lances with pennons. The regiment was ordered to convert to the weapon in 1816 in the wake of the Napoleonic Wars, having previously been a regiment of light dragoons. All in white metal, the badge is uncluttered with other impedimenta; a brass economy version was issued in 1916.

The 10th (Prince of Wales's Own Royal) Hussars

Similar in appearance to that of the 3rd Dragoon Guards, this badge simply deploys the traditional Prince of Wales's plumes, motto and coronet in bimetal, though an all-brass version, issued in 1916, also exists. The regiment's 'Royal' title was granted in 1783. The Prince of Wales referred to became King George IV in 1820, though there was no change in regimental title.

The 11th (Prince Albert's Own) Hussars

The 11th Hussars were granted the title 'Prince Albert's Own' after forming an honour guard for the Prince, when he first arrived in England in 1840. Not surprisingly, the regiment adopted his family crest – that of the House of Saxe-Coburg-Gotha – as a badge, and also its motto, *Treu und fest* ('Loyal and steadfast'). Given that other Germanic symbols were abandoned at the outbreak of war in 1914, this regiment did well to retain theirs. Its Colonel-in-Chief in 1914, the Crown Prince of Germany ('Little Willie'), was less fortunate.

The 12th (Prince of Wales's Royal) Lancers

A Lancer regiment, its badge bears the standard crossed lances of its trade, with brass and white-metal pennons; superimposed are the Prince of Wales's plumes, coronet and motto. There is an all-brass economy issue version of this badge. The regiment gained its 'Royal' status when it converted to a Lancer role in 1816.

The 13th Hussars

Two badges exist for the 13th Hussars; the larger of the two was bimetal, worn from 1898, a brass badge with crown and laurel wreath surrounding the regimental motto *Viret in aeternum* ('It flourishes forever'). The second badge is a smaller, all-brass example with the off-centre numeral '13'.

The 14th (King's) Hussars

The original badge of this regiment was a white-metal Prussian eagle (granted to the regiment in 1798, in honour of the then Duchess of York, a Prussian princess), on a brass disc. In 1915 this was replaced, not surprisingly, with an innocuous all-brass badge of Garter and royal crest. This is found in various sizes, voided and non-voided, the larger version, known as the 'cartwheel'.

The 15th (The King's) Hussars

The 15th Hussars are famed for holding the first battle honour to be granted to a British regiment, 'Emsdorf', fought in 1760. In many ways its badge resembles that adopted by the 14th Hussars in 1915, with brass Garter and white-metal royal crest. The badge carries the motto *Merebimur* ('We shall be worthy'), below the title 'XV.KH'. An all-brass economy strike was issued in 1916.

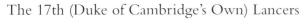

The 16th (The Queen's) Lancers

Another simple Lancer badge, this one is bimetal (though an all-brass version was issued in 1916). The 16th carried the distinction of being the first of the Lancer regiments to use the lance in action, in nineteenth-century India.

The 17th (Duke of Cambridge's Own) Lancers

This regiment possesses what is arguably the most distinctive badge (known as the 'Motto' to its soldiers) in the British Army – a white-metal skull, crossed bones and draped banner bearing the motto 'Or glory'. The badge was chosen to commemorate General Wolfe's defeat of the French at Quebec in 1759 – at the cost of his life. A brass version of the badge was issued in 1916.

The 18th (Queen Mary's Own) Hussars

Previously the Princess of Wales's Own, the title 'Queen Mary's Own' was granted to this regiment in 1910, when King George V and Queen Mary took the throne. Queen Mary was Colonel-in-Chief of the regiment at the outbreak of war. This white metal badge replaced an earlier brass version, a large badge bearing the motto *Pro Rege Pro Lege Pro Patria Conamur* ('For King, for Law, and for Country we strive')

The 19th (Queen Alexandra's Own Royal) Lancers

In 1908 the 19th Lancers became 'Queen Alexandra's Own' (having previously been 'the Princess of Wales's Own') and adopted in consequence a small white metal monogram 'A' worked with the Danish national cross (the Dannebrog), Queen Alexandra having been a Danish princess. There is a 1916 issue brass version of this badge.

The 20th Hussars

The 20th Hussars' badge was simple in conception: the Roman numeral 'XX' sandwiching the initial 'H' (for Hussars, a designation first adopted in 1862, after spells as both Dragoons and Light Dragoons). Finished all in brass, it was surmounted by a crown.

The 21st (Empress of India's) Lancers

The 21st wore crossed lances (the regiment having been designated as Lancers in 1897) with bimetal pennons on an otherwise all-brass badge. Superimposed is the monogram 'VRI', granted for services at Omdurman in 1898, when the regiment was involved in the last massed cavalry charge in history, at great cost. A wholly brass badge would be issued in 1916.

Chapter Five

CAP BADGES OF THE YEOMANRY

THE YEOMANRY was the cavalry of the Territorial Force in 1914. Yeomanry regiments had been raised through history to assist in the defence of the nation in times of crisis, particularly when there was a threat – real or imagined – from the French. The Boer War of 1899–1902 saw the raising of many more that would give good service in South Africa, styled as battalions of the 'Imperial Yeomanry'. Many of the badges used in the First World War would derive from this period, modified for the times through the simple expedient of removing the word 'Imperial'. Some Cavalry regiments of the Territorial Force were also to serve as Special Reserve Cavalry, not strictly Yeomanry, but part-time volunteers just the same, mobilised and available for service with the Cavalry in 1914. In the First World War, many of the Yeomanry regiments would have to abandon their horses and fight as dismounted infantry; the broken spur of the 74th Infantry divisional sign (page 12) expresses this with some regret.

Second Lieutenant L. E. Allan of the Westmorland and Cumberland Yeomanry, killed in action 26 April 1917.

The Royal Wiltshire Yeomanry (Prince of Wales's Own)

The badge of the most senior Yeomanry regiment (raised in 1794) is the bimetal Prince of Wales's plumes, motto and coronet; these devices were awarded to the regiment when it acted as escort to the Prince on his visit to Wales in 1863. This badge can be distinguished from the simple plumes of other regiments by its bimetal finish.

The Warwickshire Yeomanry

It took as its badge the bear and ragged staff, the ancient device of the Earls of Warwick. A number of variants are known (specifically the attachment point of the chain), and the badge is found in a number of different sizes and finishes, white metal and brass being commonest.

The Yorkshire Hussars Yeomanry (Alexandra, Princess of Wales's Own)

The badge combined the white rose of its home county with the bimetal plumes and coronet of the Prince of Wales; the title was granted after providing a detachment at Queen Victoria's Diamond Jubilee. A brass economy strike version exists.

The Nottinghamshire Yeomanry (Sherwood Rangers)

Raised originally in 1794 with men from Retford, Mansfield and Newark, the regiment was distinguished by a simple brass stringed bugle horn, the device having been associated with the Forest Rangers of Sherwood Forest. In all other respects, this resembles the white metal badge of the Oxfordshire and Buckinghamshire Light Infantry.

The Staffordshire Yeomanry (Queen's Own Royal Regiment)

In common with other Staffordshire regiments, the Staffordshire Yeomanry wore the device of the de Stafford family, the knot, here in brass topped with a crown. The 'Royal' title, conferred in 1838, derives from the regiment parading in honour of the then Princess Victoria, in 1832.

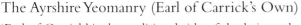

The Shropshire Yeomanry

The Shropshire Yeomanry's brass badge featured three leopards' faces on a shield, a fifteenth-century device derived from the arms of Shrewsbury, and in turn the arms of the county of Shropshire. Later versions dispensed with the shield altogether, with the three 'loggerheads' standing in the circle.

The Ayrshire Yeomanry (Earl of Carrick's Own)

'Earl of Carrick' is the traditional title of the heir to the Scottish throne (and one of the titles held by the Prince of Wales). The cap badge of this regiment was simply the arms of the Earl, a lion-headed griffin in brass; in 1915, a three-part title scroll was added, reading 'Earl of' and 'Carrick's' on the outer scrolls, and 'Ayrshire Yeomany' on the central one.

The Cheshire Yeomanry (Earl of Chester's)

In 1803 the Prince of Wales granted the use of his plumes, motto and coronet to the Cheshire Yeomanry, raised in 1797, as well as the use of one of his many titles, in this case, appropriately, the 'Earl of Chester's'. This is carried on a brass scroll with the lengthy title 'Cheshire (Earl of Chester's) Yeomanry'.

The Yorkshire Dragoons (Queen's Own)

The Yorkshire Dragoons wore the rose of Yorkshire surmounted by a crown (in white metal, brass economy strike and blackened brass versions). The regiment was granted its royal title after escorting Queen Victoria on a visit to Sheffield in 1897.

The Leicestershire Yeomanry (Prince Albert's Own)

In 1914 they wore a simple brass badge comprising the letters 'LY' within a laurel wreath bearing the battle honour 'South Africa 1900–02'. Bucking the wartime trend of discarding Germanic devices, this regiment adopted the crest of Prince Albert, that of Saxe-Coburg-Gotha, in 1915, having been given its subsidiary title in 1844. This later badge carried the titles 'Leicestershire' and 'Prince Albert's Own Yeomanry'.

The North Somerset Yeomanry

First raised in 1798, this regiment suffered disbandment in the early 1800s and gained its county affiliation in 1814. Its cap badge was based on a crowned ten-pointed white-metal star, with, at its centre, the royal cypher, surrounded by a circle bearing the motto *Arma pacis fulcra* ('Arms, the mainstay of peace').

The Duke of Lancaster's Own Yeomanry

The all-brass cap badge of this regiment is based on the red rose of Lancaster, topped, appropriately, with the ducal coronet from the Duchy of Lancaster. As it befitting a royal regiment, in 1914 the Colonel-in-Chief was King George V.

The Lanarkshire Yeomanry

The brass badge of the Lanarkshire Yeomanry is based on the fifteenth-century seal of the Royal Burgh of Lanark, a double-headed eagle and crown. The eagle holds a bell in its right claw, a device added in the sixteenth century, which alludes to the one dropped by St Kentigern (the founder of Glasgow) into the Clyde.

The Northumberland Yeomanry (Hussars)

The Northumberland Yeomanry wore a brass badge, a circle carrying the regimental title with a central castle, variously described as that of Newcastle (from the arms of the city), or Alnwick, the seat of the Dukes of Northumberland. Comparison with the actual buildings shows it to be based on the Norman keep at Newcastle. This debate continues.

The Nottinghamshire Yeomanry (South Nottinghamshire Hussars)

In common with most regiments from Nottinghamshire, the badge of the county yeomanry regiment, first adopted in 1898, draws its inspiration from the nearby Sherwood Forest, through its use of oak leaves and acorn. Examples of this effective device are found in both brass and white-metal finishes.

The Denbighshire Yeomanry

They wore simply the Prince of Wales's plumes, coronet and motto (*Ich dien* – 'I serve') in bronze finish (thereby distinguishing it from the bimetal badge of the Wiltshire Yeomanry). First raised as a single troop in 1795 in Wrexham, the regiment gained its full title in 1820, when it expanded to its full five troops of Yeomanry cavalry.

The Westmorland and Cumberland Yeomanry

The moors of these upland counties are reflected in the use of three sprigs of heather on this bronze badge – though some authorities consider the heather to be ears of wheat. In any case both devices are direct references to the association of the Yeomanry with the land. Whichever it might be, its distinctive design was the work of the second Earl of Lonsdale, who raised the unit in 1819. Officers wore a badge with a similar design, but within a circle (page 47)

The Pembroke Yeomanry (Castlemartin)

The Pembroke Yeomanry is famous for its 'Fishguard' battle honour, the only such distinction awarded for service within the British Isles, and the first to be awarded (in 1853) to a unit of volunteers within the British Army. This relates to the 1797 landing at Llanwrda, near Fishguard, of hapless French troops who were sent packing by a force of Yeomanry, and, as legend would have it, the sight of Welsh women in their shako-like tall hats. The bimetal badge has the Prince of Wales's plumes; an all-brass economy version was issued in 1916.

The Royal East Kent Yeomanry (The Duke of Connaught's Own) (Mounted Rifles)

In common with many Kentish units, the bronze (or brass) badge of this regiment bears the white horse of Kent over the motto *Invicta* ('Unconquered'), here represented within a Garter, and topped with a crown.

The Hampshire Yeomanry (Carabiniers)

The bimetal badge (and title) of this regiment derives from the regular 6th Dragoon Guards (The Carabiniers) and was adopted in 1884. That of the Hampshire Carabiniers differs in lacking the Garter, and having a white-metal Hampshire rose.

The Buckinghamshire Yeomanry (Royal Buckinghamshire Hussars)

The Royal Buckinghamshire Hussars' badge has at its centre a swan from the arms of the Dukes of Buckingham, within a circle carrying the English language motto 'Yeoman of Bucks, strike home'. Bronze, brass and even white-metal versions are known.

The Derbyshire Yeomanry

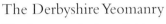

The brass cap badge of this regiment has a central rose within a laurel wreath, with the battle honour 'South Africa 1900–1901', awarded for its service as a unit of the 4th Battalion, Imperial Yeomanry during that conflict.

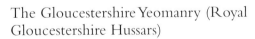

The Dorsetshire Yeomanry (Queen's Own)

The bronze Dorsetshire Yeomanry badge is in many ways similar to that of the Royal Engineers, with laurels, Garter and crown. It differs, however, in the use of the 'South Africa' battle honour on its laurels, and its central title, 'QO DorsetY'.

The Gloucestershire Yeomanry (Royal Gloucestershire Hussars)

This brass badge uses the portcullis with chains and ducal coronet derived from the arms of the Dukes of Beaufort. The regiment's first Colonel, in 1834, was the eldest son of the sixth Duke, the link with the Beaufort family being maintained through the history of the regiment.

The Hertfordshire Yeomanry

The traditional emblem of this county, a hart (mature male red deer) crossing water, is used as the badge of this regiment without embellishment, in brass. By repute, this badge is the same as the collar badge worn by the Hertfordshire Imperial Yeomanry during the South African War.

The Berkshire Yeomanry (Hungerford)

The ancient white horse cut into the chalk downs of Uffington, formerly in Berkshire, forms the simple but distinctive brass badge of this regiment, over the county title. The ancient practice of the cutting of figures in the chalk such as this was to be revived during the war by soldiers resident at Fovant, in Wiltshire, an interesting echo of the past.

The 1st County of London Yeomanry (Middlesex, The Duke of Cambridge's Hussars)

The badge of the Middlesex Yeomanry is a simple white-metal eight-pointed star. A central circle carries the motto *Pro aris et focis* ('For hearth and home') and the royal cypher. A brass version of the same badge is also recorded.

The Royal First Devon Yeomanry

They wore the simple royal crest of crown and lion, in bronze and brass, voided and solid versions. The regiment was one of two Devon Yeomanry units raised in 1798 by the charismatic Lord Rolle, MP for the county, and supporter of William Pitt the Younger. A similar badge to this was also worn by staff officers during the war.

The Suffolk Yeomanry (Duke of York's Own Loyal Suffolk Hussars)

The bimetal badge of this regiment shows the castle of Bury St Edmunds, with cross of St George flags flying from both turrets, the right-hand one flying out of true. The date 1793 reflects the year of their raising, one of the earliest of the Yeomanry regiments created for the newly declared war with France.

The Royal North Devon Hussars

The North Devon Hussars wore a simple monogram 'NDH' with crown, found in brass and bronze finishes. This regiment was the second of two raised by Lord Rolle, MP for Devon, during the eighteenth century.

The Worcestershire Yeomanry (Queen's Own Worcestershire Hussars)

This yeomanry regiment wore a distinctive bimetal badge, the white-metal centre being a sprig of pear blossom (a badge of the county, and an ancient 'field sign' for Worcester archers in the Hundred Years War), within a brass wreath, crown and title. A wartime, all-brass economy version is known (though prior to 1913 the standard badge was also all-brass).

The West Kent Yeomanry (Queen's Own)

Appropriately for this county yeomanry regiment, it wore the traditinoal prancing white horse and *Invicta* ('Unconquered'), the motto of Kent, in white metal. The same badge was worn by the Kent Cyclist battalion, Territorial Force, during its brief existence.

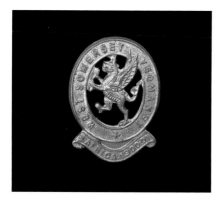

The West Somerset Yeomanry

This regiment employed the ancient badge of the kings of Wessex, the Wyvern, within an oval bearing the regimental title, in an all-brass finish. The award of the 'South Africa' battle honour, carried on an extra scroll, was in recognition of the regiment as a unit of the 7th Battalion of the Imperial Yeomanry.

The Oxfordshire Yeomanry
(Queen's Own Oxfordshire Hussars)

The Oxfordshire Yeomanry wore the cypher and crown of Queen Adelaide, consort of William IV, in white metal. The honour was granted to the regiment for furnishing a guard to the queen on her visit to Oxford, in 1835. Brass and bronze versions are known. This regiment was the first of the Yeomanry to see active service in the First World War.

The Montgomeryshire Yeomanry

Their badge was a white-metal Welsh dragon over the initials 'MY'. Raised in 1803, this regiment suffered disbandment, like many Yeomanry units, in the first half of the nineteenth century but was to supply four squadrons to the Imperial Yeomanry in South Africa towards the end of this difficult campaign.

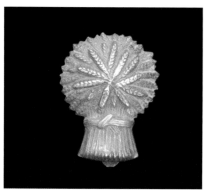

The Lothians and Border Horse

This regiment wore a simple brass wheatsheaf (known as a 'garb' in heraldic terms), a device associated with at least two ancient families from the region, and symbolising the farmlands of East Lothian. There are versions of this badge that have a smooth lower part; these are considered suspect.

The Queen's Own Royal Glasgow Yeomanry

The Glasgow Yeomanry wore the seated lion and crown crest of Scotland in brass, over a wreath of thistles. The regiment gained its 'Royal' title after supplying an escort to Queen Victoria and Prince Albert when the royal couple visited Glasgow in 1849. There is a smaller version of this badge with the icon inside a crowned circle.

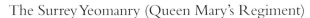

The Lancashire Hussars Yeomanry

The rose of Lancashire formed the badge of this regiment. Units of the Lancashire Hussars, originally raised in the northern towns of Bolton and Wigan in the eighteenth century, were to serve in two battalions of the Imperial Yeomanry during the South African War.

The Surrey Yeomanry (Queen Mary's Regiment)

The cap badge of this regiment displays the cypher of Queen Mary within a Garter, in both brass and white metal finishes, and in various sizes. The regiment was raised for service in the Boer War in 1901, and gained its subsidiary title in 1910, with the accession of George V to the throne.

The Fife and Forfar Yeomanry

In common with many yeomanry regiments, this one wore a county badge in white metal – the 'Thane of Fife', a knight in full armour. Raised and disbanded several times in its history, the regiment was created by the merger of the Fife Light Horse and the Forfar Light Horse in 1901. Brass versions of this badge were worn by the 14th (Fife and Forfar Yeomanry) Battalion of the Argyll and Sutherland Highlanders, dismounted cavalrymen, in the latter part of the First World War.

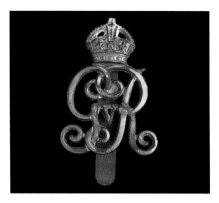

The Norfolk Yeomanry
(The King's Own Royal Regiment)

This regiment's badge is simply the royal cypher (GRV) and crown, in brass. The use of the cypher, and the regiment's 'Royal' title, was authorised by King Edward VII, in 1901, and again in 1906, when he became Colonel-in-Chief. A similar badge has also been worn by members of the Military Provost Staff Corps.

The Sussex Yeomanry

The badge of the Sussex Yeomanry was a fancy brass shield with six martlets (heraldic birds said to be without legs) – deriving from the arms of an ancient Saxon kingdom. The regiment was raised in response to the needs of the Boer War in 1901, though it had antecedents dating back to the eighteenth century.

The Glamorgan Yeomanry

In common with so many others, this yeomanry regiment was raised in the late eighteenth century to counter threats from France. As befits a Welsh regiment, it wore white-metal Prince of Wales's plumes and brass coronet, but, unusually, with the scrolls that normally bear the motto *Ich Dien* ('I Serve') being kept blank. An all-brass economy strike was issued in 1916.

The Lincolnshire Yeomanry

The Lincolnshire Yeomanry wore the shield from the arms of the City of Lincoln within laurel wreaths, in brass. First raised in 1794, the regiment served with distinction during the South African War, when it wore a white-metal version of the badge as Imperial Yeomanry. The regiment was disbanded in 1920.

The City of London Yeomanry (Rough Riders)

Raised for service in South Africa, this regiment had a large and flamboyant bimetal badge with brass wreath, crown, title and 'South Africa' battle honour. Its white-metal centre displayed the arms of the City of London, usually backed by blue cloth. Perhaps because it was too large for practical use, a simple bimetal collar badge, comprising the white metal letters 'RR' superimposed on a brass spur, was often used in its place.

The 2nd County of London Yeomanry (Westminster Dragoons)

The Westminster Dragoons wore the arms of the City of Westminster in brass (post-war, it was to become white-metal) over a scroll 'Westminster TY Dragoons', the abbreviation 'TY' standing for 'Territorial Yeomanry'. The regiment survives today.

The 3rd County of London Yeomanry (Sharpshooters)

Raised for service in the South African War, it had as its badge the numeral '3' superimposed on crossed rifles, all in brass. This replaced (in 1908) a less elegant wreath and Garter badge, with a simple 'S.S.' abbreviation at its centre.

The Bedfordshire Yeomanry

The Bedfordshire Yeomanry wore in brass an eagle from the arms of the Beauchamp family, associated with Bedford since the twelfth century, with a representation of the former Bedford Castle superimposed upon its breast. Genuine badges generally have the legs of the eagle voided.

The Essex Yeomanry

The Essex Yeomanry wore two all-brass badges during the war; both had a central shield with the three seaxes (Saxon swords) of Essex in a circle, surmounted by a crown. The first, worn until 1916, carried the motto *Decus et tutamen* ('An ornament and safeguard') in the circle; the second, worn from 1916 to 1918, with a different crown shape, had the motto moved below the circle (which now bore the regimental title) on a separate scroll. Another version with a standard king's crown appeared at the war's end.

The Northamptonshire Yeomanry

The Northamptonshire Yeomanry wore a simple white-metal depiction of a prancing white horse of Hanover, unadorned with titles or honours. The regiment dates from the latter part of the South African War (1902), though there had been other county antecedents.

The East Riding of Yorkshire Yeomanry

The East Riding Yeomanry, harking from good hunting country, wore a lean brass fox in full flight, a simple design with no further embellishment – though officers' versions are known in precious metals. A bimetal version appeared with a slyer-looking fox, and the hunting term 'Forrard', in 1920.

The First Lovat's Scouts Yeomanry

Raised in 1900 by Lord Lovat, chief of Clan Fraser, this regiment in 1914 had as its white metal badge the stag's head crest of the clan, surrounded by a circle bearing the title 'Lovat's Scouts' (changed, after 1922, to 'Lovats Scouts'. Other versions are known, including examples with brass finishes, and variation in the shapes of the stag's antlers. After 1922, the regimental title changed to 'Lovats Scouts.

The Scottish Horse

The central device of this white-metal badge is the Scottish saltire over an oval, bearing the regimental title and date of raising (1900), flanked by wreaths of juniper (left) and laurel (right). A brass version is also known.

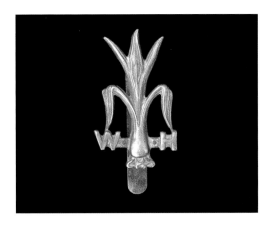

The Welsh Horse Yeomanry

This was one of two Welsh regiments raised in the first years of the war, this one in 1914 (the other being the Welsh Guards in 1915); both would take the ancient symbol of the leek as their badge – the Welsh Horse distinguished by the initials 'W.H.' flanking it.

SPECIAL RESERVE CAVALRY

The King Edward's Horse (The King's Oversea Dominions Regiment)

This regiment was raised in 1901 from volunteers from the dominions and was originally styled the 'King's Colonials', before taking its new name in 1910. On its brass badge, laurel wreaths bear the names of the dominions, and the motto *Regi adsumus coloni* ('Colonials venture for the King').

The 2nd King Edward's Horse

Raised in 1914, the 2nd King Edward's Horse bore a brass badge similar in conception to that of The King Edward's Horse, but slightly larger, and with the addition of the title 'Crown Colonies', the date 1914, and with the motto 'Empire and liberty', replacing the Latin version of its namesake.

The North Irish Horse

This regiment was derived from Imperial Yeomanry antecedents; in 1908, as there was to be no Territorial Force raised in Ireland, it was transferred to the Special Reserve. In practical terms, the brass 'angel harp' with title scroll worn by the regiment was very similar to the badge of the regular 8th (Royal Irish) Hussars.

The South Irish Horse

The South Irish Horse wore another Irish symbol, a brass shamrock, bearing the initials 'SIH'. As with its northern Irish equivalent, the South Irish Horse (also originally part of the Imperial Yeomanry) was transferred to the Special Reserve on the formation of the Territorial Force in 1908. It would be disbanded in 1922, with the formation of the Irish Free State.

Men of the Bedfordshire Yeomanry relax for the camera. Most wear stiff service-dress caps with the distinctive eagle cap badge of this regiment, as well as the leather bandoliers worn by mounted soldiers.

Chapter Six

CAP BADGES OF THE INFANTRY

THE INFANTRY is composed of several groups with different origins. The Foot Guards were formed to provide a close guard for the monarch and are considered an elite. The majority, the Infantry of the Line, are the regiments that fought originally in the linear formations that typified warfare in the eighteenth century. That century saw additional specialists that remain, in name, to this day: Light Infantry trained as skirmishers, and Grenadiers, operating as lead assault troops. The development of the Baker rifle led also to new Rifle regiments. Successors to these specialists would become integral to the British Army. An order of precedence set by tradition would rank the five regiments of Foot Guards above the county regiments of Infantry of the Line, the Rifles sitting towards the end of this list.

Unknown rifleman in the Rifle Brigade, c. 1915.

As well as the standard infantry regiments, there are also the Royal Marines, controlled by the Admiralty. At this point they were divided into both infantry and artillery roles. According to military tradition, when serving with the Army, the Royal Marines ranked in precedence after The Royal Berkshire Regiment. Other mariners were also to see service as infantrymen – Royal Naval Reservists put into khaki as the men of the Royal Naval Division. Divided into battalions, they served in Gallipoli and on the Western Front. Other unlikely units also served as infantry: the dismounted cavalry of the Household Battalion and of many Yeomanry regiments. Their badges have already been described.

THE FOOT GUARDS

Guards' cap badges, for Guardsmen at least, are relatively uncomplicated brass affairs, mostly taking their inspiration from the orders of chivalry, as described below; those for senior NCOs and officers are grander, often finished in precious metals. These are less often encountered.

The Grenadier Guards

The name 'Grenadier Guards' dates back to 1815, when the First Regiment of Foot Guards (originally raised in 1660) defeated the Grenadiers of Napoleon's Imperial Guard at Waterloo. In honour of the act, the Prince Regent granted the regiment the right to adopt the title and brass grenade, with the brass flaming grenade as its insignia.

The Coldstream Guards

The Coldstream Guards were first raised in 1650, part of the New Model Army, and were later taken into the service of the King, after formally laying down their arms in 1661. This act placed them second in precedence to the Grenadiers. The badge (known regimentally as a 'cap star') is the star of the Order of the Garter and the Garter itself, which was granted to the regiment by William III in 1696.

The Scots Guards

The Scots Guards (formally raised in 1660, but dating back at least another ten years) wore the star of the Order of the Thistle, as its 'cap star' with its central thistle device and motto, *Nemo me impune lacessit* ('No one may touch me with impunity') in all-brass for other ranks.

The Irish Guards

The Irish Guards were raised in 1900 'to commemorate the actions of Irish regiments' in South Africa. In common with the Coldstream and Scots Guards, the brass 'cap star' badge of the Irish Guards is based on an order of chivalry, the Order of St Patrick, with its motto *Quis separabit* ('Who will separate us?').

The Welsh Guards

Raised in wartime at the request of George V, in February 1915, the Welsh Guards quickly took their position alongside the other national contingents. In reference to ancient Welsh feats of arms, they took the leek as their badge, in brass, an echo of the use of the plant as a field sign by Welsh soldiers during the Middle Ages.

The Guards Machine Gun Battalion

Formed in 1917, the Guards Machine Gun Battalion (of the Guards Division), otherwise known as the 'Machine Gun Guards', had a five-pointed white metal star, its points as bullets. Devices representing the five regiments of Foot Guards (grenade, rose, thistle, shamrock and leek) were located between the points, with the apposite motto *Quinque juncta in uno* ('Five joined in one') surrounding the intertwined and reversed monogram 'GMG'. The date 1916 refers to the development of the Guards Machine Gun training centre.

The Guards Machine Gun Regiment

In February 1918 the Guards Machine Gun Regiment was formed. Three Household Cavalry regiments were converted to a machine-gun role, forming the 1st to 3rd Battalions; the 4th was the existing Guards Machine Gun Battalion. Its badge consists of the monogram 'GMGR' within the garter, crossed Vickers machine guns, and regimental title, in brass.

The Guards Officer Cadet Battalion

The battalion served to train and supply officers to the Foot Guards and Household Cavalry. The outer enamel edge links together the initials of the host units: the 1st and 2nd Life Guards, The Royal Horse Guards and the five regiments of Foot Guards. The links between these is further emphasised by the central chain surrounding the royal cypher.

INFANTRY OF THE LINE

Cap badges of the infantry regiments, created following the Cardwell–Childers reforms of 1881, display devices that link the regiments with their historic past. Unlike those of the Guards, special senior NCO badges are rare; officers' badges are generally bronze examples of the standard version.

The Royal Scots (Lothian Regiment)

With an unbroken record of service dating back to 1633, and claiming to go back even further, this regiment is nicknamed 'Pontius Pilate's Bodyguard'. They wore a white-metal star from the Order of the Thistle. A red backing was used by the 1st Battalion, a green one by the 2nd. A brass economy strike exists.

The Queen's (Royal West Surrey Regiment)

This regiment was raised in 1661. The Paschal (holy) lamb was part of the arms of Queen Catherine of Braganza, the wife of Charles II, its use confirmed by the Royal Warrant of 1751. The badge was issued in all-brass in 1916.

The Buffs (East Kent Regiment)

The regiment is so named because of their buff facing colours, worn with full dress. The Buffs' brass dragon, confirmed in 1751, may have been sourced from the arms of Elizabeth I and is thought to have been awarded to the regiment by Queen Anne in 1707.

The King's Own (Royal Lancaster Regiment)

This is another ancient regiment permitted to wear a distinctive badge by order of the Royal Warrant of 1751. The lion of England may have been granted by William III, as the regiment was the first to join him on his arrival in England in 1688. The title 'The King's Own' was granted by George I.

The Northumberland Fusiliers

This is the most senior Fusilier regiment of the British Army. The ball of the traditional flaming grenade borne by the corps carries a depiction of St George and the Dragon, possibly adopted when the regiment joined the British Army after service with William of Orange in Ireland.

The Royal Warwickshire Regiment

The antelope of their bimetal cap badge is associated with the regiment's service overseas during the War of the Spanish Succession, possibly deriving from the standard of a Spanish regiment beaten at the Battle of Saragossa in 1710.

Captain R. B. Gibbons, Royal Warwickshire Regiment, killed in action on 3 September 1917.

The Royal Fusiliers (City of London Regiment)

The Royal Fusiliers were originally raised as a protective force for the artillery. Their distinctively shaped brass flaming grenade badge bore the Garter with a central five-petalled rose, with a crown above. The Rose and Garter device is thought to have been borrowed from that traditionally carried on cannon barrels.

The King's (Liverpool Regiment)

The white horse of Hanover was an honour granted to the regiment by George I following its operations against Jacobite rebels in 1715, a device confirmed to the regiment in 1751. The badge is bimetal, but an all-brass issue appeared in 1916.

Pte F. Morris of the King's Liverpools, killed in action, 30 July 1916.

The Norfolk Regiment

The white-metal figure of Britannia within a wreath was awarded to the regiment by Queen Anne following the Battle of Almanza in 1707, and was confirmed to the regiment in 1799. It is a unique distinction. There is an all-brass economy strike of this badge.

The Lincolnshire Regiment

The Lincolnshire Regiment wore the white-metal sphinx and Old English 'Egypt' title tablet, awarded for operations against the French in 1802. A brass scroll bears the regimental county distinction, 'Lincolnshire'. An all-brass economy version of this badge was issued in 1916. Officers had their own, distinctive, badge: an eight-pointed star with a sphinx at its centre.

The Devonshire Regiment

The Devonshire Regiment wore a bimetal star, with a representation of Exeter Castle in white metal over the motto *Semper fidelis* ('Always faithful'), in commemoration of the defence of the city, by armed forebears, during the English Civil War. There was an all-brass version issued in 1916.

The Suffolk Regiment

The regiment had as its central device a white-metal castle and key of Gibraltar (awarded for the defence of the Rock during the siege of 1779–83), within a circle carrying the motto *Montis insignia Calpe* (literally 'The badge of the Rock of Gibraltar'). There is an all-brass economy strike of this badge.

The Prince Albert's (Somerset Light Infantry)

In white metal (a brass version appeared in 1916), this badge incorporates the bugle horn of the Light Infantry, a distinction gained in 1822. Several honours were awarded for the defence of Jellalabad during the First Afghan War (1839–42), the royal title and initials 'PA', a mural (walled) crown signifying the defence of the city, and the battle honour itself.

The Prince of Wales's Own (West Yorkshire Regiment)

Their badge was the white horse of Hanover, over a brass regimental title, similar in many ways to the badge of the 3rd (King's Own) Hussars. Originally raised in Kent, the regiment had several regional titles before finally becoming a Yorkshire regiment in 1881. An all-brass, 1916-issue version exists of this bimetal badge.

Private John Irvine Hargraves of the West Yorkshire Regiment, who died from bronchial pneumonia at Étaples four days after the Armistice in 1918 – the result of being gassed. His brother, Harry Hargraves (page 6), was to survive the war.

The East Yorkshire Regiment

The East Yorkshires wore an eight-pointed brass star with a central white-metal rose of Yorkshire within a laurel wreath, a device that derived from at least two militias. An all-brass version was issued in 1916. This particular badge was the property of Private Albert Phillips, who stamped it with his regimental number (6060), and who served in Flanders from February 1915.

The Bedfordshire Regiment

The regiment wore a white-metal star (from the Order of the Garter) with a Maltese cross (associated with the first Colonel of the regiment). At the centre of the badge, within a Garter is a deer (a hart) crossing a ford, a device taken from the Hertford Militia, which joined the regiment following the Cardwell-Childers reforms in 1881. There was an all-brass version of this badge.

The Leicestershire Regiment

They wore a distinctive bimetal badge (a 1916 all-brass version was issued). It bears a brass 'royal tiger' (green with gold stripes on the regimental colour) with the white-metal honour scroll 'Hindoostan', both granted to the regiment (then 17th Foot) for services in India during 1804–23.

The Royal Irish Regiment

The Royal Irish Regiment was originally raised in Ireland, part of Oliver Cromwell's Independent Garrisons. Its royal title was granted by William III in honour of the regiment's part in storming the castle at Namur in 1695, and the conferment of the crown and harp also dates from this time. The regiment was disbanded in 1922 with the formation of the Irish Free State.

The Lancashire Fusiliers

The Lancashire Fusiliers is another regiment that bears the sphinx (awarded for actions against the French in Egypt in 1801). The device is displayed on the traditional brass grenade of the Fusiliers and is surrounded by a wreath awarded in honour of the regiment's heroism at the Battle of Minden in 1759.

The Royal Scots Fusiliers

The Royal Scots Fusiliers and Royal Scots Greys were both raised to counter threats from the Covenanters, who opposed the Scottish government in the seventeenth century. The regiment wore a large brass grenade, worn in the glengarry (and identical with its nineteenth-century version), with the royal arms superimposed, taken from the Royal Warrant of 1751.

Alexandra, Princess of Wales's Own (Yorkshire Regiment)

The cap badge of this regiment is based on its association with Princess Alexandra, then Princess of Wales, in 1875. The central device of this white-metal badge (first used in 1908; an all-brass version was issued in 1916) is an 'A' interwoven with a Danish cross (the Dannebrog), bearing the date 1875, and topped with the Princess's coronet.

Soldier of the Yorkshire Regiment; his two sleeve chevrons indicate two years' service overseas.

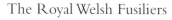

The Cheshire Regiment

The Cheshires wore a badge that comprised an eight-pointed white-metal star (there is an all-brass version), with a brass acorn and oak leaves at its centre. The foliage is said to have been granted by George II, for service in saving him from capture at the Battle of Dettingen (1743), but no direct evidence exists of the regiment being present at the battle. A number of unsatisfactory theories have been advanced to explain this anomaly.

The Royal Welsh Fusiliers

This regiment wore a bimetal Fusilier grenade distinguished by the Prince of Wales's plume, motto and coronet, granted to the regiment in 1751. An all-brass version was issued in 1916. In 1922, 'Welsh' became 'Welch', an archaic spelling. The sphinx was granted for action in Egypt in 1801, but this device was carried only on the regimental colours.

The South Wales Borderers

This distinctive badge marries the white-metal sphinx and 'Egypt' honours from 1801 with a brass wreath of immortelles, awarded by Queen Victoria for the actions of the 24th Foot in the Zulu War of 1879. A brass economy strike was issued in 1916.

The King's Own Scottish Borderers

They were first raised in Edinburgh in 1689. The central device is a depiction of Edinburgh Castle over the Scottish saltire. Above is the motto *In veritate religionis confido* ('In true religion is my trust'); below, *Nisi Dominus frustra* ('Unless the Lord is with me all is in vain') – both mottoes associated with the city.

The Cameronians (Scottish Rifles)

Equipped with the bugle horn common to Rifle regiments, the main device of this white-metal badge is a mullet (five-pointed star) taken from the coat of arms of the first Colonel of the regiment in 1689, the Earl of Angus, a member of the Douglas family. The regiment, raised from Covenanters, was named after the religious reformer Richard Cameron.

The Royal Inniskilling Fusiliers

As a Fusilier regiment, its badge is based on a brass flaming grenade; superimposed upon the grenade is a white-metal castle of Inniskilling, relating to the defence of the castle when besieged by King James II, in 1689. The flag of St George flies to the left from the central turret; from 1934, the flag flew to the right. An all-brass version was issued in 1916.

The Gloucestershire Regiment

The Gloucestershire Regiment wore a white-metal badge (issued in brass in 1916) comprising a sphinx over the 'Egypt' honour, awarded for actions against the French in 1801. An unusual dress distinction was the wearing of a smaller brass badge (consisting of sphinx, 'Egypt' honour and wreath) at the back of their caps. Known as the back badge, it relates to the conduct of the regiment in fighting the French back to back at the Battle of Alexandria, and was awarded in 1830.

The Worcestershire Regiment

The eight-pointed star of this brass badge derives from the Order of the Garter, upon which is a Garter circle with central royal lion. The motto 'Firm' is thought to relate to the regiment's 'firmness' during the assault on the fortress of Bangalore, in 1791.

A soldier in the Worcestershire Regiment

The East Lancashire Regiment

This bimetal (all-brass in 1916) badge incorporates a white-metal sphinx (from service in Egypt against the French in 1801), above the red rose of Lancashire. The regiment's association with Lancashire dates back to the Cardwell-Childers reforms, when it was first titled the 'West Lancashire Regiment', its name change following a few weeks later.

The East Surrey Regiment

The device at the heart of this bimetal badge is derived mostly from the arms of Guildford, Surrey's county town (star, castle and lion), but is reputed to have three tiny salmon (on the central turret), from the arms of Kingston-upon-Thames. An all-brass economy strike of this badge was issued in 1916.

The Duke of Cornwall's Light Infantry

The Light Infantry bugle is topped with a ducal coronet in this white-metal badge. The regiment was awarded the honour of being Light Infantry in 1857, after its defence of Lucknow during the Indian Mutiny, and was the last regiment to be designated a representative of this specialist corps.

Second Lieutenant Chard of the Duke of Cornwall's Light Infantry – he wears bronzed DCLI badges.

The Duke of Wellington's (West Riding Regiment)

This regiment wore the arms of the Iron Duke himself, Wellington having served as Colonel of the 33rd Foot, and as a junior officer with the 76th foot, both being linked during the Cardwell-Childers reforms. The Duke's motto, *Virtutis fortuna comes* ('Fortune favours the brave') is apposite. The badge is bimetal, but an all-brass version was issued in 1916.

The Border Regiment

This white-metal badge is unusual in many ways. On a star from the Garter, and cross from the Order of the Bath, the battle honour 'Arroyo dos Molinos' is borne only by this regiment. This relates to a battle in the Peninsular War in 1811 when the French 34th Regiment – the Border Regiment then also being the 34th Foot – was captured in its entirety. The red and white centre of the badge reflects the red and white shako pom-poms of their French opposite number. The laurel wreath relates to action at the Battle of Fontenoy in 1745; the dragon and title 'China' were awarded for service in the China War of 1840–2.

The Royal Sussex Regiment

The Royal Sussex wore a bimetal (all-brass in 1916) badge with the white-metal star of the Order of the Garter. Behind are the plumes (granted to the regiment in 1901) that were taken from the French Regiment of Royal Roussillon, whom the 35th Foot defeated under Wolfe at Quebec in 1759.

The Hampshire Regiment

Commonly known as the 'Cat and Cabbage', this bimetal badge (there was an all-brass issue) has the royal tiger, awarded for action in India during 1805–26, particularly at the siege of Asseerghur; below is the Hampshire rose, by repute granted to the city of Winchester by Henry V on his way to Agincourt.

The South Staffordshire Regiment

The South Staffs wore the white-metal knot of the de Stafford family (which also appears in the county badge of Staffordshire) in a bimetal badge finished with a brass title scroll. An all-brass economy version of the badge was issued in 1916. The regiment has been associated with its home county since the late eighteenth century.

A soldier in the South Staffordshire Regiment.

The Dorsetshire Regiment

The sphinx on this badge was derived from service in Egypt, the regiment having captured Fort Marabout from the French. The castle and key of Gibraltar were granted for service on the Rock during the siege of 1779–83, while the title *Primus in Indis* ('First in India') relates to the fact that they were the first crown regiment to serve in the subcontinent, famously serving under Clive at the Battle of Plassey. The badge is bimetal, though an all-brass economy strike was also issued.

The Prince of Wales's Volunteers (South Lancashire Regiment)

The title 'Prince of Wales's Volunteers' and the plume, coronet and motto are derived from the 82nd Foot, the sphinx from the actions of the 42nd Foot. The regiments linked during the Cardwell-Childers reforms. Originally bimetal, this badge was issued in brass in 1916.

Above: A soldier in the South Lancashire Regiment.

Left: Private Charlie Marshall, Welsh Regiment, pictured in 1915.

The Welsh Regiment

They wore a bimetal badge comprising a white-metal plume, motto (*Ich dien* – 'I serve') and brass coronet of the Prince of Wales. There was an all-brass economy strike issue of this badge in 1916. The spelling 'Welsh' reverted to the archaic version 'Welch' in 1920.

The Black Watch (Royal Highlanders)

Though wearing just a distinctive 'red hackle' awarded for actions in the American Revolutionary War, the regiment had as its badge a handsome, diamond-cut white-metal (brass in 1916) star of the Order of the Thistle, with St Andrew at its centre. The Black Watch being veterans of the 1801 Egyptian campaign, a sphinx is present. The motto *Nemo me impune lacesset* ('No one may touch me with impunity') has the variant spelling *lacessit* and is also derived from the Order. The name 'Black Watch' may hark back to the beginnings of the regiment; raised in 1739 to suppress rebellious Highlanders, it was distinguished from the 'red soldiers' by its sombre 'Government' tartan.

Soldiers of the Black Watch, c. 1917. In most cases, a red feather hackle, awarded to the regiment in 1822, was worn in place of the elaborate cap badge.

Soldier of the Oxfordshire and Buckinghamshire Light Infantry.

The Oxfordshire and Buckinghamshire Light Infantry

The simple white-metal bugle horn reflects the seniority of this Light Infantry regiment, which adopted this role in 1803. Its constituent parts (the 44th and 56th Foot) both served as Light Infantry during the Peninsular War. A similar badge, in brass, was worn by the Nottinghamshire Yeomanry (page 48)

The Essex Regiment

This is another veteran regiment of the Egyptian campaign of 1801 and the siege of Gibraltar (1779–82, an earlier date in this case). Their bimetal (all-brass in 1916) cap badge is adorned with the appropriate devices: the sphinx, and the castle and key of the Rock. The badge is finished with a wreath of oak leaves, traditionally associated with Charles II's escape by hiding in the 'Royal Oak'.

Captain J. L. Whalley of the Essex Regiment (wearing an officer's bronzed version of the Essex badge). He died of wounds on 30 December 1917.

Soldier in the Nottinghamshire and Derbyshire Regiment.

The Sherwood Foresters (Nottinghamshire and Derbyshire Regiment)

The stag within the oak-leaf device relates to Nottingham and to Sherwood Forest; the stag forms part of the arms of the city. The badge was originally bimetal, with white stag, cross and oak leaves over a brass title scroll, but an all-brass economy version was issued in 1916.

The Loyal North Lancashire Regiment

The red rose of Lancashire (petal uppermost) is the main device of this bimetal badge, capped with the royal crest of the Duchy of Lancaster. The 'Loyal' title was derived from the motto of the Earl of Lindsey, who raised the 81st Foot, originally the 'Loyal Lincoln Volunteers'.

The Northamptonshire Regiment

This bimetal badge bore the castle and key of Gibraltar (relating to the siege in 1779–83) and also wore the battle honour 'Talavera', when against all odds the regiment protected the high ground during this Peninsular War battle in July 1809. An all-brass issue was made in 1916.

Princess Charlotte of Wales's (Royal Berkshire Regiment)

They wore the dragon in honour of their actions during the China War of 1840–2; the 'Royal' title was granted for work at the Battle of Tofrek, in the Sudan, in 1884–5. Other distinguished service was as marines during the Battle of Copenhagen in 1801; officers wear a coil of rope in addition to the dragon as a mark of distinction, an allusion to this distinguished service.

The Queen's Own (Royal West Kent Regiment)

The rearing white horse depicted on this badge is associated with this regiment's home county, as is the motto, *Invicta* ('Unconquered'), in Old English script. Both are derived from the ancient kingdom of Kent, the device being used by Kentish warriors for centuries. A brass economy version of this white-metal badge was issued in 1916.

The King's Own (Yorkshire Light Infantry)

Theirs was the smallest cap badge in the British Army, just 33 mm wide and 20 mm high; the largest, that of the Argyll and Sutherland Highlanders, measured 78 by 55 mm. The King's Own became a Light Infantry regiment in 1809 and wore a bimetal bugle in the form of a French horn, with the white rose of Yorkshire. A brass economy strike was issued in 1916.

The King's (Shropshire Light Infantry)

This regiment was designated Light Infantry in 1808 and gained its royal title in 1821. As with all Light Infantry regiments, the KSLI wore the white-metal bugle, with the brass initials of the regiment between the strings. An all-brass version was issued in 1916.

The Duke of Cambridge's Own (Middlesex Regiment)

The cypher of George, Duke of Cambridge, is interlaced and reversed at the centre of this bimetal badge, below his ducal coronet and the Prince of Wales's plumes. The battle honour 'Albuhera', fought in May 1811, earned the regiment the nickname 'the Diehards'. An all-brass version was issued in 1916.

A soldier in the Middlesex Regiment; his 1916 pattern soft cap chinstrap has been braided, a fashion of the day.

The King's Royal Rifle Corps

The KRRC wore a black Maltese cross with the motto *Celer et audax* ('Swift and bold'), granted for service under Wolfe in Canada in 1759. The red backing is in tune with the red piping, collars and plumes of the full-dress rifle-green uniform. As a Rifle regiment, it carried no colours, so some of its battle honours are displayed on the cross. This was the inspiration for the badges of at least four London Territorial battalions, with which it can be confused.

The Duke of Edinburgh's (Wiltshire Regiment)

The regiment became the 'Duke of Edinburgh's' in 1874. The brass Maltese cross worn carries at its centre the monogram 'AEA', from Alfred Ernest Albert, second son of Queen Victoria, then Duke of Edinburgh; the ducal coronet is his.

The Manchester Regiment

The Manchesters wore bimetal arms of the City of Manchester, with the motto *Concilio et labor* ('Wisdom and effort') – sometimes disparagingly referred to as the 'Tram Conductor's Badge'. The regiment adopted an older device, the fleur-de-lys, in 1923. No economy version is known, though an all-brass solid version of the badge was issued to 'Manchester Pals' (page 108).

A soldier in the Manchester Regiment

The Prince of Wales's (North Staffordshire Regiment)

In common with other regiments from this county, this corps wore the de Stafford knot, this time in brass with white-metal Prince of Wales's plumes, motto and brass coronet, the use of the Prince of Wales's title having been granted in 1876. A brass version was issued in 1916.

The York and Lancaster Regiment

This is another bimetal 'Cat and Cabbage' badge, issued in all-brass in 1916. It comprised the royal tiger and the union rose, appropriate because the title of the regiment refers to the union of the two royal houses, the regiment having been firmly based in Yorkshire (though the ducal coronet comes from the Duchy of Lancaster).

Soldier in the York and Lancaster Regiment.

The Durham Light Infantry

In common with the other six Light Infantry regiments, the DLI wore the white-metal (brass in 1916) Light Infantry bugle, here decorated with a leaf motif. The regiment had been associated with Durham since the late eighteenth century, and a Light Infantry corps since 1808.

The Highland Light Infantry

The badge is based on the star of the Order of the Thistle, with the Light Infantry bugle and regimental monogram at its centre. The battle honour 'Assaye' (found on both short and long scrolls) and the elephant were awarded for services in India against the Mahrattas in 1803. There is an all-brass 1916-issue version of this badge.

The Seaforth Highlanders
(Ross-shire Buffs, The Duke of Albany's)

The stag's head was sourced from the arms of the Earls of Seaforth, who wore the Mackenzie crest. This derives from the clansman who saved King Alexander II of Scotland from an infuriated stag in 1266, severing the head of the beast (which is why it has no neck). The Gaelic motto *Cuidich'n righ* ('Help the king') refers to this ancient act.

The Gordon Highlanders

The white-metal badge derives its stag from the crest of the Duke of Gordon, who raised the regiment in 1794, and who also gave it its ducal coronet and motto *Bydand*, often spelt *By dand* ('Watchful'). An all-brass version was issued in 1916.

The Queen's Own Cameron Highlanders

This regiment wore a representation of St Andrew and the saltire. Badges without the title scroll beneath St Andrew are pre-war, though it has been suggested that these were still worn by old soldiers during the conflict. There is an all-brass version of this white-metal badge.

The Royal Irish Rifles

The original badge of the regiment was blackened, but a white-metal version of it was adopted in 1913. The motto *Quis separabit* ('Who shall separate us?') is from the Order of St Patrick; the harp and coronet are also associated with that order.

Princess Victoria's (Royal Irish Fusiliers)

The Prince of Wales's plumes and the Fusilier title came from the 87th Foot; the coronet (that of Princess, later Queen Victoria) relates to the 89th. The regiments were amalgamated in 1881. The coronet was issued separately, and has fixing loops, but it is often found fixed to the grenade.

The Connaught Rangers

They wore the harp of Erin (as opposed to the more usual 'angel', or Maid of Erin, harp seen in Irish cap badges) surmounted by a crown in brass. The badge is relatively slender, and additional strengthening is seen behind the crown on original examples. The regiment was disbanded with the creation of the Irish Free State in 1922.

The Princess Louise's (Argyll and Sutherland Highlanders)

Measuring 78 mm by 55 mm, this is the largest cap badge in the British Army – a flamboyant white-metal object with, at its centre, the cypher of Princess Louise (intertwined and reversed), below her coronet. At its centre, in voided and solid versions, is a boar's head from the crest of the Argyll family, and a cat from the Sutherland family.

The Prince of Wales's Leinster Regiment (Royal Canadians)

The 100th Foot was originally raised in Canada to assist during the Indian Mutiny. The typical, bimetal badge had angular motto scrolls; curved scrolls are also known, suggesting reuse of the die from the Welsh Regiment badge. A brass version was issued in 1916. The regiment was disbanded with the creation of the Irish Free State in 1922.

The Royal Munster Fusiliers

The Munsters were derived from two former regiments of the East India Company, transferred to the British Army in 1858 and amalgamated in 1881; this explains the royal tiger, for service in India. Bimetal, the badge was issued in an all-brass 'economy' version in 1916. The regiment was disbanded with the creation of the Irish Free State in 1922.

The Royal Dublin Fusiliers

The Dublin Fusiliers also had East India Company antecedents, the 101st bringing the royal tiger, and the 103rd the elephant. The badge was bimetal, but there is also an all-brass 'economy' strike, issued in 1916. The regiment was disbanded with the creation of the Irish Free State in 1922.

The Rifle Brigade (The Prince Consort's Own)

The Rifle Brigade was raised as a Corps of Riflemen armed with the Baker rifle in 1800. Numbered 95th Foot in 1802, it saw distinguished service at Waterloo. In 1816 its number was abandoned and it became simply 'The Rifle Brigade'. This rifle regiment carried no colours: its battle honours are represented on the arms of the Maltese cross, and on fourteen honour scrolls on the laurel wreaths. More were added later for service in the First World War.

THE ROYAL MARINES

In 1914 (as they had been since 1855) the Royal Marines were composed of two branches, *The Royal Marine Light Infantry* (RMLI) (left) and *The Royal Marine Artillery* (RMA). Both would serve on land and at sea. The globe of the RMLI's brass badge was awarded to the corps in 1827 by George IV (recognising their global service), for the capture of Belleisle in the Bay of Biscay in 1761. In the First World War the RMLI served with the Royal Naval Division on land. The gunners of the RMA wore the distinctive flaming grenade badge, also in brass (page 89).

In 1917 *The Royal Marine Labour Corps* was formed from men derived from the Army Service Corps for service at home. Its rare brass badge, consisting of a ship in full sail atop the globe, is commonly reproduced (below right).

THE ROYAL NAVAL DIVISION

The Royal Naval Division was formed as infantry in 1914 from men of the Royal Naval Volunteer Reserve and saw service at Antwerp in the early part of the war. Officers and NCOs of the division used naval ranks throughout. Eight battalions were raised, named after famous admirals. Two of them were disbanded after Gallipoli – the 3rd (Benbow) and 4th (Collingwood) – in order to supply reinforcements for the others. The 9th (Machine Gun) Battalion was raised in 1916. Cap badges were not issued until late in 1916, as previously the men had worn either Wolseley helmets (in Gallipoli) or Nelson caps with the cap tally 'Royal Naval Division'. The badges were mostly (notably apart from that of the 9th) made by Gaunt's and are distinguished by a small plaque bearing the name 'J.R.Gaunt London' on the reverse, as well as loop fittings. All RND badges are commonly reproduced.

Period cap with Royal Naval Division tally; this was worn prior to the introduction of cap badges in 1916.

The 1st (Drake) Battalion RND

Bimetal, the badge depicts a white-metal sailing ship on a brass globe, with the motto *Auxilio divino* ('By divine aid'), taken from the arms of Sir Francis Drake (1540–96). It should be two separate words on genuine badges such as this one, as well as braze holes and a Gaunt plaque to the rear.

The 2nd (Hawke) Battalion RND

The majority of RND badges are based on devices from the arms of famous admirals. This badge comprises a hawk (with fleur-de-lys) and the motto 'Strike', from the arms of Admiral Hawke (1705–81), victor of the Battle of Quiberon Bay against the French in 1759.

The 5th (Nelson) Battalion RND

The battalion was named for Admiral Horatio Nelson (1758–1805), the victor of Trafalgar. This brass badge depicts his flagship, HMS *Victory*, in full sail. There are at least two versions, most notably one smaller with different script, though its authenticity is disputed.

The 6th (Howe) Battalion RND

Admiral Howe (1726–99) was famous for his actions against the French and in the American War of Independence. The badge depicts a brass naval coronet; those considered genuine are usually 'voided', and, like all RND badges, commonly bear the 'J R Gaunt London' tablet, to the rear.

The 7th (Hood) Battalion RND

Like Admiral Howe, Admiral Hood (1724–1816) was famed for his actions in the French and American Revolutionary Wars. Based on his arms, the badge depicts a Cornish chough and anchor from his crest, with the motto 'Steady'.

The 8th (Anson) Battalion RND

Admiral Anson (1697–1762) circumnavigated the world. This badge comprises a spear and coronet and the motto *Nil desperandum* ('Never despair') from the crest of the Earls of Lichfield, members of the Anson family. The spear is a weak feature of this badge and is commonly found with strengthening applied to the rear.

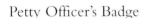

The 9th (Machine Gun) Battalion RND

Reputedly made in RND workshops, this badge combines the crossed-guns cap badge of the Machine Gun Corps with a curved 'R.N.D.' shoulder title brazed or soldered to it. It is argued that genuine badges have evidence of the fixing loops removed from the title; this example shows this, and the crude attachment.

Petty Officer's Badge

RND Petty Officers wore a distinctive, large blackened brass badge, consisting of a disc with fouled anchor and rope, surmounted by a crown. Officers wore a fouled anchor with crown and laurels, also in blackened finish.

Chapter Seven

CAP BADGES OF THE TERRITORIAL AND SERVICE BATTALIONS

THE CREATION of the Territorial Force in 1908 – drawing deeply on Volunteer battalion antecedents – brought with it a variety of badges that distinguish smaller, more local units that had been shepherded into the fold of the county regiments. Bringing rich traditions, many have their own distinctive badges; others simply employed the Regular badge, often blackened if they were Rifle battalions, or with blanked-out honour scrolls. A good many other Territorials simply used the badge of the Regulars, where this was non-contentious. Several of them, given a Cyclist role, are identified in their badges by the tool of their trade – the bicycle wheel.

Service battalions arose from Lord Kitchener's distrust of the Territorial Force. Impatient, autocratic and controlling, Kitchener had the foresight to recognise that the war would be a long one – and sought to increase the numbers of men joining the army as volunteers, in tranches of 100,000. These men would form the basis, initially at least, of the Service battalions; an ever-expanding resource of men attached to the Regular county regiments. With the patriotic fervour – and the energies of local dignitaries such as Lord Derby in Liverpool and Manchester – came the raising of local Pals" or 'City' battalions – fed, clothed and equipped by the local purse. It is not surprising that these battalions would wear their own locally designed cap badges and other insignia.

TERRITORIAL BATTALIONS

Not all Territorial battalions would have their own, distinctive badge; a great many others would have a modified version of the Regular badge. Represented here are those with distinctive insignia; many are scarce.

Two soldiers of the Liverpool Scottish, pictured in Blackpool.

The 4th and 5th Battalions, The Royal Scots (Queen's Edinburgh Rifles) TF

Their badge was a white-metal star of the Order of the Thistle, similar to that worn by officers of the Regular battlions, with a central thistle device and motto, *Nemo me impune lacessit* ('No one shall touch me with impunity'). A bugle horn indicates their Rifles status.

The 5th Battalion, The Queen's (Royal West Surrey Regiment) TF

The battalion wore a 'Paschal lamb' badge in blackened-brass finish consistent with their origin as a Rifle battalion.

The 5th, 7th and 9th Battalions, The King's (Liverpool Regiment) TF

All wore a Regular pattern Hanoverian horse and title badge, but with blackened-brass finish, typical of Rifle battalions (5th Battalion), or with white-metal finish, worn typically by the pre-Territorial era volunteers (7th and 9th Battalions). Both are illustrated.

The 6th (Rifle) Battalion, King's (Liverpool Regiment) TF

This battalion wore a distinctive bugle horn (typical of Rifle regiments), beneath the Lancastrian rose, in blackened-brass finish; this was worn with a red backing. Officers of this battalion wore the same devices as collar badges.

The 8th (Irish) Battalion, The King's (Liverpool Regiment) TF

The blackened-brass badge of the 8th Irish featured an angel harp and shamrocks, with the battalion title scroll. The example illustrated has had its black finish worn off with use. In 1939, the badge was issued with a slightly different title, in white metal.

The 10th (Scottish) Battalion, The King's (Liverpool Regiment) TF

The handsome white-metal glengarry badge worn by this battalion bears the regimental title and white horse of Hanover in high relief over the traditional Scottish symbols of a saltire and thistles in two sprays, curving upwards.

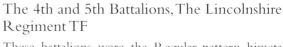

The 4th and 5th Battalions, The Lincolnshire Regiment TF

These battalions wore the Regular-pattern bimetal badge, comprising white-metal sphinx and brass title scroll, but differing, in common with many Territorial battalions, in possessing a blank 'Egypt' plinth below the sphinx.

The 4th and 5th Battalions, The Devonshire Regiment TF

They wore the Regular-pattern badge (a star with a representation of Exeter Castle), but in either blackened-brass Rifle (4th) or white-metal Volunteer (5th) finishes. Both are illustrated.

The 4th, 5th and 6th (Cyclist) Battalions, The Suffolk Regiment TF

Their bimetal badge shows the castle of the county town of Bury St Edmunds, replacing that of Gibraltar (its key removed), within a narrow blank circle (which normally would have carried the motto of the Rock). An all-brass economy strike version was issued in 1916.

The 4th and 5th Battalions, Prince Albert's (Somerset Light Infantry) TF

Both battalions wore a badge that was similar to the Regular pattern, consisting of a white-metal bugle with the initials of Prince Albert, but with 'South Africa 1900–01' replacing 'Jellalabad' – though the mural crown (associated with the defence of that city) remains.

The 7th and 8th Battalions, The Prince of Wales's Own (West Yorkshire Regiment) (Leeds Rifles) TF

As both were Rifle battalions, they wore blackened badges based broadly on that worn by the Rifle Brigade, though differing through the use of the central title 'Leeds Rifles', the absence of the Brigade's extensive honours, and with title scrolls appropriate to the battalion.

The 5th (Cyclist) Battalion, The East Yorkshire Regiment TF

The badge worn by the East Yorkshire Cyclists spurned the use of the cycle wheel, and instead is of Regular pattern, but in blackened-brass finish.

The 4th and 5th Battalions, The Leicestershire Regiment TF

The Leicestershire Territorials wore a bimetal 'royal tiger' badge, but without the upper 'Hindoostan' scroll – a paradoxical decision, given that both were awarded to the Regular battalions as a battle honour. An all-brass version was issued in 1916.

The 5th, 6th, 7th and 8th Battalions, The Lancashire Fusiliers TF

These battalions used a Regular-pattern bimetal badge, comprising a white-metal title scroll beneath the traditional brass grenade of Fusilier regiments. The grenade bears a superimposed sphinx, but, in common with most Territorials, it lacks the honour 'Egypt'.

The 1st, 2nd and 3rd Brecknockshire Battalions, The South Wales Borderers TF

Officially numbered 1/1st, 2/1st and 3/1st battalions, all wore a distinctive Welsh dragon badge in all-brass, over the title 'Brecknockshire'. The 1st Battalion served in Aden and India; the others were home Service battalions.

The 5th Battalion, The Cameronians (Scottish Rifles) TF

This battalion wore a badge that, in part, resembled the one worn by Regular battalions. However, it is noticeably smaller and has several differences of design: a complete circle of thistles, and a mullet and bugle within. The numeral '5' is found within the strings of the bugle.

The 4th (City of Bristol), 5th and 6th Battalions, The Gloucestershire Regiment TF

All three Gloucestershire Territorial battalions wore the large sphinx badge over a title scroll, though with a blank 'Egypt' battle honour tablet. The City of Bristol Battalion (a Rifles unit) wore the badge in blackened-brass finish, the 5th and 6th Battalions had the usual white-metal finish, as illustrated.

The 4th and 5th Battalions, The East Lancashire Regiment TF

Both battalions wore the Regular-pattern bimetal badge, comprising a white-metal sphinx over a brass Lancashire rose within a white-metal wreath; it is distinguished by the usual blank 'Egypt' tablet beneath the sphinx. An all-brass economy issue was struck in 1916.

The 6th Battalion, The East Surrey Regiment TF

This battalion wore a distinctive, large black-finish Maltese cross bearing the 'South Africa 1900–1902' battle honour, with the arms of Guildford displayed on a star at its centre, surrounded by the battalion title. Illustrated is the officers' version, basically the same, but with burnished high points.

The 4th (Cumberland and Westmorland) and 5th (Cumberland) Battalions, The Border Regiment TF

They used white-metal badges, bare of honours other than 'South Africa 1900–02', which were based on the Regular one (though with a numeral replacing the red and white centre), with appropriate title scrolls. The 4th Battalion badge illustrated, with subdued relief, is a copy.

The 5th (Cinque Ports) Battalion, The Royal Sussex Regiment TF

The all-brass badge of the Cinque Ports Battalion was based on that of the Regulars, employing the Maltese cross over the plumes won from the French Regiment of Royal Roussillon, but with the arms of the Cinque Ports (Hastings in Sussex, New Romney, Hythe, Dover and Sandwich in Kent) at its centre.

The 6th (Duke of Connaught's Own) Battalion, The Hampshire Regiment TF

The Duke of Connaught's Own wore a bimetal badge, with a brass Hampshire rose within a white-metal wreath topped with a ducal coronet, and with a brass title. The Duke of Connaught became this battalion's honorary Colonel in 1903, when it was then the 3rd Volunteer Battalion.

The 7th Battalion, The Hampshire Regiment TF

This distinctive all-brass voided badge comprises a 'dog gauge' within a brass wreath. The gauge (by repute a stirrup that once belonged to the medieval King William Rufus) was used some centuries ago to restrict the access of the large dogs of commoners to the New Forest – thereby protecting hunting rights.

The 8th (Isle of Wight Rifles, 'Princess Beatrice's') Battalion, The Hampshire Regiment TF

This badge found in brass and blackened-brass finishes features the central tower of Carisbrooke Castle, surrounded by a laurel wreath and with the 'South Africa' battle honour. Princess Beatrice's husband, Prince Henry of Battenburg, was the honorary Colonel of the battalion.

The 9th (Cyclist) Battalion, The Hampshire Regiment TF

In common with most Cyclist battalions, the cap badge of this battalion reproduces a bicycle wheel, with a Hampshire rose at its centre, with the battalion title on a scroll beneath it. A solid, non-voided and enamelled version of this badge is known.

The 4th Battalion, The Dorsetshire Regiment TF

For all intents and purposes, the 4th battalion wore the Regular bimetal badge, consisting of a brass wreath and title, with a white-metal castle and key of Gibraltar over the motto *Primus in Indis* ('First in India') with the sphinx above, differing through its blank 'Marabout' battle honour tablet.

The 4th and 5th Battalions, The Prince of Wales's Volunteers (South Lancashire Regiment) TF

These battalions wore badges based on the Regular pattern, comprising regimental titles and wreath, within which are Prince of Wales's plumes, coronet and motto, over a sphinx with the usual blank 'Egypt' tablet. This is found in bimetal (4th Battalion, illustrated; an all-brass economy version was issued in 1916) and blackened-brass (5th Battalion) finishes.

The 7th (Cyclist) Battalion, The Welsh Regiment TF

This battalion scorned the usual cycle-wheel device of most Cyclist battalions and instead wore the Regular badge, consisting of the Prince of Wales's plumes, coronet and motto, over 'The Welsh' title scroll, but differing with its blackened-brass finish.

The 4th (City of Dundee), 5th (Angus & Dundee), 6th (Perthshire) and 7th (Fife) Battalions, The Black Watch (Royal Highlanders) TF

These battalions wore the usual handsome Regular pattern white-metal badge, consisting of a star based on that of the Order of the Thistle, with St Andrew and the motto *Nemo me impune lacessit* (or *lacesset*), meaning 'No one may touch me with impunity' at its centre, but without the sphinx.

The 1st, 2nd and 3rd Buckinghamshire Battalions, The Oxfordshire and Buckinghamshire Light Infantry TF

Officially titled the 1/1st, 2/1st and 3/1st Buckinghamshire Battalions, all wore a black Maltese cross with the swan of Buckinghamshire placed centrally within the battalion title, a device derived from the arms of the Dukes of Buckingham. The 1/1st battalion served in France and Italy, the others as home defence during the First World War.

The 4th, 5th, 6th and 7th Battalions and 8th (Cyclist) Battalion, The Essex Regiment TF

These battalions used the Regular-pattern bimetal badge comprising brass oak wreath over white-metal regimental title, with a central castle and key of Gibraltar, on top of which is the usual sphinx with blank 'Egypt' plinth. In this form it was worn by the 8th Battalion (illustrated); the 4th–7th Battalions had an additional brass 'South Africa 1900–02' honour scroll attached to the bottom of the badge. An all-brass economy version of this badge was issued in 1916.

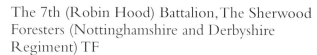

The 7th (Robin Hood) Battalion, The Sherwood Foresters (Nottinghamshire and Derbyshire Regiment) TF

This battalion wore a 'Rifle Brigade' pattern badge consisting of a Maltese cross with central bugle, surrounded by the title 'The Robin Hoods' in blackened brass (also in white metal), with the honour 'South Africa 1900–02' on the lower three arms of the cross.

The 4th Battalion, The Northamptonshire Regiment TF

The 4th Northants used the Regular bimetal badge, with white-metal castle and key of Gibraltar within a wreath, with brass 'Northamptonshire' title, but with the upper ('Gibraltar') and lower ('Talavera') honour scrolls left blank. An all-brass economy version was issued in 1916.

The 7th, 8th, 9th and 10th Battalions, The Duke of Cambridge's Own (Middlesex Regiment) TF

These battalions wore the Regular pattern bimetal badge, consisting of a brass wreath enclosing bimetal Prince of Wales's plumes, coronet and motto over the Duke of Cambridge's cypher, and white-metal regimental title, but with the 'Albuhera' honour scroll either left blank (in the 7th, 8th and 9th Battalions; an all-brass 1916 issue version exists) or replaced with the honour 'South Africa 1900–02' (the 10th Battalion, illustrated).

The 4th Battalion, The Duke of Edinburgh's (Wiltshire Regiment) TF

The battalion wore the Regular cross (known heraldically as a 'cross pattée') badge bearing the coronet and cypher ('AEA', Alfred Ernest Albert) of the Duke of Edinburgh, over the regimental title, but in blackened-brass finish.

The 7th Battalion, The Manchester Regiment TF

The 7th Manchesters wore a brass, floriated fleur-de-lys. The fleur-de-lys, later adopted post-war by the Regular battalions of the Manchester Regiment, is a device associated with the actions of the regiment against the French at Martinique during the nineteenth century.

The 6th Battalion, The Durham Light Infantry TF

The 6th DLI wore a Regular pattern badge, though in the blackened-brass finish illustrated, comprising the usual Light Infantry bugle horn, this time bearing a floriated pattern, with the initials 'DLI' between the strings. Officers wore bronze versions with an additional 'South Africa 1900–02' honour scroll beneath.

The 5th (City of Glasgow), 6th (City of Glasgow), 7th (Blythswood) and 8th (Lanark) Battalions, The Highland Light Infantry TF

These battalions wore the Regular pattern badge, but with the 'Assaye' honour scroll either left blank (used by the 5th, 7th and 8th Battalions until 1916) in both short and long versions, or replaced with 'South Africa 1900–02' (the 6th Battalion alone, then all four battalions from 1916). A brass economy strike version was issued in 1916.

Captain G. L. McEwan of the 6th Battalion, Highland Light Infantry, who died of wounds on 21 July 1915, while serving in Gallipoli.

The 9th (Glasgow Highlanders) Battalion, The Highland Light Infantry TF

This battalion had a white-metal 'Black Watch' pattern badge, comprising a star based on that of the Order of the Thistle, with St Andrew and the motto *Nemo me impune lacessit* (or *lacesset*) at its centre, but with 'Glasgow Highlanders' and '9th HLI' replacing the title scrolls of the original. Somewhat illogically, this badge possesses a sphinx, while that of the Territorial battalions of the Black Watch itself did not.

The 5th (Sutherland and Caithness) Battalion, The Seaforth Highlanders (Ross-shire Buffs, The Duke of Albany's) TF

They wore a white-metal wild cat from the arms of the Dukes of Sutherland within a circular Celtic strap bearing the motto *Sans peur* ('Without fear'). This is commonly found with a pin fixing. After 1920 the Celtic strap became a simple circle.

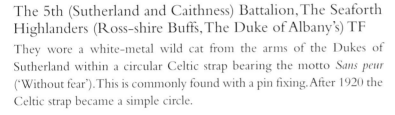

The 8th (Argyllshire) Battalion, Princess Louise's (Argyll and Sutherland Highlanders) TF

The 8th A.S.H. used the flamboyant white-metal Regular pattern badge with, on a field of thistles, the central cypher of Princess Louise (intertwined and reversed), below her coronet, with boar's head and wild cat. The badge differs with the addition of a scroll bearing the title '8th Bn A. & S.H.'. The badge is rare and the example illustrated is a copy.

The Northern Cyclist Battalion TF

Independent, but associated with the Northumberland Fusiliers, this battalion wore the usual simple but effective cycle-wheel design adopted by most Cyclists, but with crossed-rifles and is found in both brass and bronze finishes.

The Highland Cyclist Battalion TF

The Highland Cyclists wore a badge of 'Black Watch' pattern, a star based on that of the Order of the Thistle, with St Andrew and the motto *Nemo me impune lacessit* at its centre, and lacking the sphinx, with 'Highland Cyclist' and 'Battalion T.F.' replacing the title scrolls of the original.

Private H. A. Taylor, Kent Cyclist Battalion.

The Kent Cyclist Battalion TF

This battalion wore the white horse of Kent badge and the motto *Invicta* ('Unconquered') of the West Kent Yeomanry, in white metal. The battalion was to be used as part of home defence, patrolling the coastline.

The Huntingdonshire Cyclist Battalion TF

This battalion wore a springing stag derived from the county arms, over the title 'Huntingdonshire', in brass. The battalion was raised early in 1914, after some campaigning, the county not having its own Territorial battalions.

SERVICE BATTALIONS

Most Service battalions wore the cap badge of the Regular battalion, sometimes distinguished by separate shoulder titles, or even collar badges. Those battalions with distinctive cap badges are given below.

The 20th–23rd (Service) Battalions, The Northumberland Fusiliers (1st, 2nd, 3rd and 4th Tyneside Scottish)

These battalions were raised by the Lord Mayor of Newcastle in 1914. They wore no fewer than four patterns of cap badge, all of which incorporated a castle, a lion with a banner inscribed with a St Andrew's cross, and sprays of thistles. The first, issued in 1914, was a circular Celtic strap; this was replaced by a larger glengarry badge based on the saltire in January 1915, with a lion standing with both feet firmly on the tower. This badge used a stout pin fastening. The next variant appeared later in 1915, the lion raising one of his legs. This was replaced again in early 1916 by the final variant, which had the lion emerging from the turret. Both of these used loops. There is a brass version, though this is suspect.

14th–16th (Service) Battalions, The Royal Warwickshire Regiment (1st–3rd Birmingham)

The Birmingham City Battalions were raised in 1914 by the Lord Mayor of Birmingham. They wore an enamel badge before the issue of uniform (page 11). Ultimately, they wore a badge similar to that of the Regular battalions, but with some noticeable differences. The most obvious is the shorter 'Royal Warwickshire' title scroll, and the additional scroll beneath, carrying the battalion designation (1st, 2nd, 3rd), these two die-struck as one piece. A more subtle distinction is the noticeable hairs on the antelope's pelt, absent on both the regular badge – and most fakes (page 36).

25th (Service) Battalion, The Royal Fusiliers (City of London Regiment) (Frontiersmen)

The 25th Battalion was formed from a body of men (and later women) known as the Legion of Frontiersmen, an organisation raised in 1904 'to assist the state in times of need'. Offered to the War Office, at first in an irregular capacity, they were turned down initially, but accepted as the 25th Battalion of the Royal Fusiliers in January 1915. Three badges are known. The first was made in a local garage, adding a hand-engraved, sheet-brass scroll to a Grenadier Guards badge. The second pattern was cast 'in theatre' (the 25th served in East Africa, exclusively) and was worn in the puggaree of the Wolseley helmet. The one illustrated (left) belonged to Private Edgar Wilkes, who was discharged sick in 1916 – over 80 per cent would succumb to the ravages of disease. Fakes of this badge are noticeably lighter, with thinner lettering. A final pattern, gilt with enamels, is possibly a post-war 'old comrades' badge (right).

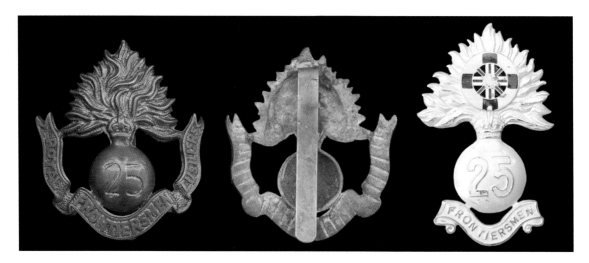

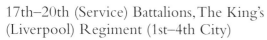

38th, 39th and 40th (Service) Battalions, The Royal Fusiliers (City of London Regiment)

Raised from Jewish volunteers in January 1918 for service in Palestine, they wore the Menorah (a ceremonial candlestick with seven branches), with the Hebrew motto *Kadimah* ('Eastward'). Fakes have noticeably different tablets in the base.

17th–20th (Service) Battalions, The King's (Liverpool) Regiment (1st–4th City)

The 'Liverpool Pals' were raised by Lord Derby in August to October 1914. The first men to join these four battalions were given a hallmarked silver cap badge, a representation of the crest of Lord Derby. Later issues were in brass and bronze; this badge is widely reproduced.

15th and 17th (Service) Battalions, The Princess of Wales's Own (West Yorkshire Regiment) (1st and 2nd Leeds)

Raised by the Lord Mayor of Leeds in September and December 1914 respectively, these two battalions of the 'Leeds Pals' wore the arms of the city as a cap badge, in brass (officers' silver versions are known). Fakes have relatively slender owls with longer legs, and with crude detailing on the shield (page 36).

13th (Service) Battalion, The East Surrey Regiment (Wandsworth)

Raised in June 1915 by the Mayor and Borough of Wandsworth, the battalion took as a badge (designed by the town clerk) the standard East Surrey pattern, with the arms of Wandsworth replacing those of Guildford. Genuine badges have the local maker's mark, 'F. Starr, Putney', behind its white-metal slider.

11th (Service) Battalion, The Border Regiment (Lonsdale)

The battalion was raised by the Earl of Lonsdale in October 1914; officers (at least) received a hallmarked silver badge with the Lonsdale crest over appropriate title scrolls. This example is brooched. Subsequent issues were in brass, and the genuine article should have a 'J. R. Gaunt London' maker's plaque to the rear.

18th (Service) Battalion, The Duke of Cambridge's Own (Middlesex Regiment) (1st Public Works Pioneers)

Raised at Alexandra Palace by Lieutenant-Colonel John Ward MP, initially from council workers, it was to serve as a Pioneer battalion and wore the standard badge, with the addition of an additional brass title scroll. This badge has been heavily copied.

16th–23rd (Service) Battalions, The Manchester Regiment (1st–7th City)

The Manchester Pals wore an all-brass or bronze, solid non-voided version of the regular badge, with loop fittings. Typically, the striking of this badge is seen to be 'indistinct'. Bimetal versions, with slider instead of loop fittings, are also known, but their authenticity is disputed.

14th (Service) Battalion, The Royal Irish Rifles (Young Citizens)

This battalion was raised from the paramilitary Young Citizens' Volunteer Corps of the Ulster Volunteer Force (UVF), raised originally to resist home rule, but offered for government service in 1914. A range of insignia was worn that derived from its founding organisation, the shamrock and red hand of Ulster being prominent on brass and white-metal badges.

THE TERRITORIAL REGIMENTS

The largest independent units within the Territorial Force were the Territorial regiments, raised in smaller counties not capable of supporting a two-battalion Regular regiment. Nevertheless, these units would see active recruitment through the war.

The Honourable Artillery Company

The HAC can be traced back to 1537, and Henry VIII; it is the oldest surviving military unit with a continuous history. It has two branches. The Artillery wore a badge similar to that of the Royal Artillery, a nine-pounder cannon, but with the motto *Arma pacis fulcra* ('Arms, the mainstay of peace'). The HAC was granted the right to wear the same uniform as the Grenadier Guards by William IV; the infantry badge is of Grenadier Guards pattern, but with the monogram 'HAC'.

Unknown officer of the HAC (Infantry).

The Hertfordshire Regiment

First raised as Rifle Volunteers in 1859, the regiment wore a hart (mature male deer) within a circle, topped with a crown, in brass in 1908; there are two versions based on the spread of the beast's antlers, wide and narrow, associated presumably with different manufacturers' dies. A solid, non-voided economy strike is known for this badge.

The Monmouthshire Regiment

The regiment was derived from Rifle Volunteers first raised in 1859. From 1908 the regiment wore a white-metal (1st Battalion) or brass (2nd Battalion) Welsh dragon, unembellished with titles (though officers of the 2nd Battalion wore a titled badge, with a different dragon). After the war, the 1st Battalion badge was as illustrated on page 29, with battle honours and Flanders poppies.

The Herefordshire Regiment

Raised as Rifle Volunteers in 1860, from 1908 the regiment wore a bimetal badge, comprising a white-metal lion holding a short sword in its raised right paw, based on the arms of the City of Hereford – granted to the city by King Richard I (the Lionheart) – over the title 'Herefordshire'.

The Cambridgeshire Regiment

Cambridgeshire Rifle Volunteers were raised in 1860–1. When the regiment was formed in 1908, it wore a bimetal badge (with an all-brass 1916 economy issue), consisting of Cambridge Castle with the arms of Ely in white metal, with brass title. Two versions are known, one with the spelling 'Cambridgshire', based presumably on two different manufacturers' dies. Some authorities consider this to be an error of Second World War vintage.

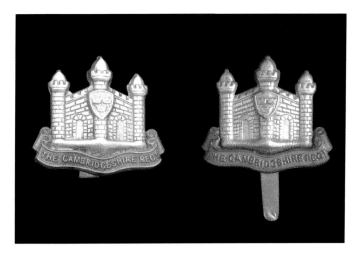

The Royal Militia of the Island of Jersey

First raised at least as long ago as the fourteenth century, it wore from 1902 a shield from the arms of Jersey, over a horizontal saltire (from the flag of Jersey), in brass. The arms comprise three leopards, facing left; examples exist with them facing right, thought to have been manufactured during the Second World War from collar badges, which are issued in facing pairs.

The Royal Guernsey Light Infantry

Raised in the fourteenth century, it was to develop into the Royal Guernsey Militia, with three regiments of Light Infantry. From 1901, they wore a traditional Light Infantry bugle, in brass, the strings finished in a fleur-de-lys finial, over the regimental title.

THE LONDON REGIMENT (TF)

The largest of the Territorial regiments, the London Regiment was formed in 1908. It was intended originally to have twenty-eight battalions (though the 26th and 27th would remain unfilled). Many Rifle battalions would have badges inspired by the King's Royal Rifle Corps or the Rifle Brigade, from their origins as volunteer battalions of these corps.

1st–4th (City of London) Battalions (Royal Fusiliers)

Originally formed as Volunteer battalions of the Royal Fusiliers, they wore the badge of their parent corps, as illustrated on page 67.

5th (City of London) Battalion (London Rifle Brigade)

The battalion wore a white-metal badge with crossed sword and mace; the royal arms were central, above the arms of the City of London. The motto *Primus in urbe* ('First in the city') refers to their Victorian forebears – the 1st London Rifle Volunteers, raised in 1859.

6th (City of London) Battalion (City of London Rifles)

The battalion was known from the severity of its badge as the 'Cast Iron Sixth'. This black cap badge was of King's Royal Rifle Corps design, lacking battle honours other than 'South Africa 1900–02', and bearing the motto of the City of London, *Domine dirige nos* ('Lord direct us')

Soldier of the 6th Londons (the 'Cast Iron Sixth').

7th (City of London) Battalion

Known as the 'Shiny Seventh', the battalion wore a simple, slender bimetal brass grenade with an applied white-metal numeral '7'; the inspiration for this was from the battalion's forebears, the 3rd London Rifle Volunteers, who wore a similar badge with the number '3'.

8th (City of London) Battalion (Post Office Rifles)

The Post Office Rifles wore a white-metal badge of Rifle Brigade type. The honours 'Egypt 1882' (granted in honour of men from the battalion, then the 24th Middlesex Rifle Volunteers, who volunteered to serve as the Army Post Office during the campaign) and 'South Africa 1899–1902' are unique among Territorial battalions.

9th (County of London) Battalion (Queen Victoria's Rifles)

This is another black King's Royal Rifle Corps pattern badge, again lacking honours other than the standard 'South Africa' honour, here on a tablet beneath the crown. At the centre of the badge, voided, is a depiction of St George slaying the dragon.

10th (County of London) Battalion (Hackney)

The 10th wore a brass badge depicting a tower from the arms of Hackney over a star and within a laurel wreath, the tower being arguably redundant owing to its motto *Justitia turris nostra* ('Justice is our fortress'). The title scroll bears the designation 'Tenth London Hackney'.

11th (County of London) Battalion (Finsbury Rifles)

The battalion wore a smaller King's Royal Rifle Corps type black Maltese cross badge, with the 'South Africa 1900–02' battle honour. It bears the title 'Finsbury Rifles' at its centre, and the motto *Pro aris et focis* ('For hearth and home') on the arms of the cross.

12th (County of London) Battalion (The Rangers)

Another black King's Royal Rifle Corps-inspired Maltese cross design, this badge has a regimental title scroll, 'The Rangers' added below the cross. The motto 'Excel' is a play on the number borne by its forebears – the 40th Middlesex Rifle Volunteers, 'XL' being forty in Roman numerals.

13th (County of London) Battalion (Princess Louise's Kensington)

The arms of Kensington appear on an eight-pointed star, in brass. The battalion was granted the use of Princess Louise's title in 1914. The war artist Eric Kennington, who served with it during the war, depicts the battalion in his painting *The Kensingtons at Laventie*, which features the cap badge prominently.

14th (County of London) Battalion (London Scottish)

The London Scottish wore a white-metal glengarry badge, with central lion and the saltire, and motto 'Strike sure', as well as the 'South Africa' battle honour. It was the first Territorial infantry battalion in action, in October 1914 in the Ypres Salient. The regimental monument is at Messines and depicts the cap badge on a Celtic cross.

15th (County of London) Battalion (Prince of Wales's Own Civil Service Rifles)

The Civil Service Rifles wore sombre black Prince of Wales's plumes, coronet and *Ich dien* ('I serve') motto. First formed in 1798 as 'The Bank of England Volunteers', they were granted their royal title in 1898.

16th (County of London) Battalion (Queen's Westminster Rifles)

The Queen's Westminsters wore a black Maltese cross, again inspired by that of the King's Royal Rifle Corps, with a portcullis from the arms of the City of Westminster at its centre. There are voided and solid versions of this badge. After the war, this battalion was merged with the 15th.

17th (County of London) Battalion (Poplar and Stepney Rifles)

The Rifle Brigade pattern badge of this battalion (in white-metal, brass and blackened finishes) is devoid of honours other than 'South Africa 1900–02'. At the centre of the badge, the title 'Rifle Brigade' displays its origins.

18th (County of London) Battalion (The London Irish Rifles)

This battalion wore a simple black (white-metal, post-war) harp of Erin and crown. First formed with many other Rifle Volunteers in 1859, with the perceived threat from France, they saw action during the Battle of Loos in September 1915.

19th (County of London) Battalion (St Pancras)

This is another badge based on that of the Rifle Brigade (in brass, white-metal and black finishes). It bears the number 'XIX' and 'South Africa' honour, most often with the dates '1900–02', but versions are known with the date '1899–1902', produced in error.

20th (County of London) Battalion (Blackheath and Woolwich)

The battalion was raised originally in 1859 as 3rd and 4th Kent Rifle Volunteers. With the formation of the Territorial Force and the London Regiment in 1908, the battalion took as its cap badge the white horse of the Royal West Kent Regiment, over the motto *Invicta* ('Unconquered'), with the addition of a battalion title scroll beneath.

21st (County of London) Battalion (1st Surrey Rifles)

Raised as the 1st Surrey Rifles in 1803, this battalion took as its badge in 1908 a small black Maltese cross, bearing the 'South Africa' honour and the date '1803' (relating to the raising of the Surrey Rifles), and the motto scroll *Concordia victrix* ('Unity is victorious').

22nd and 24th (County of London) Battalions (The Queen's)

Derived from the 6th and 8th Surrey Rifle Volunteers, raised in 1859, these battalions wore the bimetal badge of The Queen's (Royal West Surrey Regiment).

23rd (County of London) Battalion

In common with other battalions, this one was derived from the 7th and 26th Surrey Volunteer Rifles, merged in 1880. The battalion's bimetal (all-brass in 1916) badge was based on that of the East Surrey Regiment, with the brass arms of Guildford within a circle carrying the 'South Africa' battle honour, on a white-metal star.

28th (County of London) Battalion (Artists Rifles)

The central device of this badge was the twin heads of Mars and Minerva, the gods of war and the arts respectively, designed by W. C. Wyon RA. There are two patterns: one simply bore the title 'Artists' (in brass, white metal and black); the other (in brass and white metal) was larger, the title having the additional word 'Rifles'.

1st/1st London Divisional Cyclist Company

A short-lived independent company of the 58th and later 56th (London) Divisions. Raised in 1916, the company wore a brass badge based on the 25th Battalion of the London Regiment, with the arms of the City of London. Later, it became a unit of the Army Cyclist Corps.

25th (County of London) Battalion (Cyclists)

The first Cyclist battalion to be organised, as the 26th Middlesex (Cyclist) Rifle Corps in 1888, it wore a bicycle wheel within a circle and wreath, a central numeral '25', and the motto *Tenax et audax* ('Tenacious and bold'), in a brass finish.

The Inns of Court Officer Training Corps

Originally intended as the 27th Battalion, this actually served during the war as an Officer Training Corps. The all-brass badge incorporated four shields: Lincoln's Inn (top); Inner Temple (right); Gray's Inn (bottom); and Middle Temple (left).

Chapter Eight

CAP BADGES OF THE ARMS AND SERVICES

The senior support arms – those men called upon to engage in fighting – are the component units of the Royal Regiment of Artillery and the Corps of Royal Engineers, both deserving their motto *Ubique* ('Everywhere') and their right of precedence before the Foot Guards. With the advent of new technology – the aeroplane, bicycle, machine gun and tank – other arms were developed to deploy these inventions.

Additional to the support arms were the support services, required to keep the army fully functioning in its war-winning purpose. These services exist to support the well-being of the soldier, and to supply the logistical demands of the army. Though often unsung, the work of these men – and latterly women – is rightly encapsulated in functional designs for the cap badges of their services.

SUPPORT ARMS

The support arms accompany the Cavalry and Infantry wherever they are in action.

Mounted soldier of the Royal Army Medical Corps.

Royal Horse Artillery, Royal Field Artillery and Royal Garrison Artillery

All three units of artillery wore the same badge, in brass, depicting a nine-pounder smoothbore field gun from the late nineteenth century. Some examples have a revolving wheel, but there seems to be no clear explanation as to why this feature exists; others have strengthening applied to the rear of the badge (page 34). Above the gun is the *de facto* battle honour *Ubique* ('Everywhere'); beneath, the second part of the motto *Quo fas et gloria ducunt* ('Wherever right and glory lead'). A solid economy strike appeared in 1916 (bottom left). Territorial gunners wore the same badge as their regular comrades, *Ubique* being replaced by a spray of laurels (bottom right).

Soldier of the Royal Field Artillery, c. 1917.

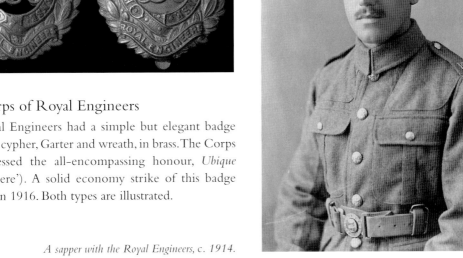

The Corps of Royal Engineers

The Royal Engineers had a simple but elegant badge with royal cypher, Garter and wreath, in brass. The Corps also possessed the all-encompassing honour, *Ubique* ('everywhere'). A solid economy strike of this badge appeared in 1916. Both types are illustrated.

A sapper with the Royal Engineers, c. 1914.

The Royal Flying Corps

Developed from the Royal Engineers in 1912, the Corps wore the monogram RFC in a wreath, with brass finish (bronze for officers). This was the inspiration for the long-lived Royal Air Force badge, issued in 1919. A solid economy strike of the RFC badge was issued in 1916. Both are illustrated.

Lieutenant G. F. Pearson, an observer in the Royal Flying Corps, transferred from the Royal Fusiliers. He was to be killed on 10 July 1917.

The Army Cyclist Corps

Raised in 1914, taking over divisional Cyclist companies, the Corps's badge was the cycle wheel (in twelve- and sixteen-spoke versions) and crossed rifles, in brass and bronze. There is a solid non-voided 1916 economy version of this badge.

The Motor Machine Gun Service

Was formed early in the war, and encompassed mobile units mounted on motorcycles. The badge, designed in 1915 by Major Philip Jupe DSO, was of brass crossed Vickers machine guns, with the white metal title 'rocker' 'MMG' attached by lugs; other examples have the title applied directly to its face. Both are illustrated, based on the two gun patterns described below.

A soldier of the Machine Gun Corps, c. 1917.

The Machine Gun Corps

Raised in 1916, the corps took the badge of the Motor Machine Gun Service, omitting the MMG title. Several variants are known, based, it is suggested, on different machine gun patterns; the two illustrated show a pre-war Vickers-Maxim, with non-standard rearsight (left), and the more usual Mark 1 Vickers (right). The Corps was disbanded in 1922.

The Tank Corps

The Tank Corps was developed from the 'Heavy Branch' of the Machine Gun Corps in 1917 and wore an effective 'tank and wreath' design, with the regimental title in brass (bronze for officers).

Royal Naval Air Service Armoured Car Section

Under Admiralty control, this unit was sent overseas early in the war, serving with the Royal Naval Division in Antwerp. The badge, in bronze, features a Rolls-Royce armoured car and may actually have been worn on the collar, rather than the cap.

SUPPORT SERVICES

These services, not fighting arms, sustained the army in the field.

The Army Service Corps

Providing transport and a myriad of other services, this Corps had the monogram ASC within a Garter, set upon an eight-pointed star. There is a solid, economy strike version of this badge, issued in 1916. Both types are illustrated; there are many variants of this badge.

The Army Remount Service

Raised during the war, the Army Remount Service sourced and supplied horses for the army. It had two badges: one in brass with a horse, horseshoe and whip; the other bimetal, with a prancing horse and royal cypher.

The Labour Corps

The Labour Corps was formed in January 1917, with men no longer fit for front-line service. Initially, men joining the Corps were to wear the 'general service' royal arms in brass, but in October 1918 a new badge was approved, comprising in brass a rifle, shovel and pick piled together, with the motto *Labor omnia vincit* ('Work conquers all'). This would become the badge of the Pioneer Corps in the Second World War and beyond.

The Royal Army Medical Corps

Responsible for the provision of medical services, the men of this Corps wore the rod and serpent of Aesculapius (the Greek god of medicine) within a laurel wreath, and topped with a crown, in all-brass.

The Army Ordnance Corps

Responsible for equipment supply and maintenance, the Corps bore the arms of the Board of Ordnance (three cannons and three cannon balls) on a shield, over the Corps title, all in brass.

The Military Police

Responsible for policing within the army, the Military Police had two branches, composed of experienced men. *The Military Mounted Police* was most senior, with a brass badge of cypher and wreath. *The Military Foot Police* wore the royal crest and title scroll in bimetal. After the war the two branches merged and wore the badge of the senior partner.

The Army Chaplains' Department

The Department was composed of officers of 'relative rank'. Christian chaplains wore the black metal cross illustrated (its blackened finish worn off); Jewish chaplains wore the Star of David. Both badges were topped with a crown.

The Army Pay Corps

The badge of this Corps, responsible for the pay of the troops, was simply the brass monogram APC, beneath a crown. Victorian versions of this badge were larger, and devoid of the crown.

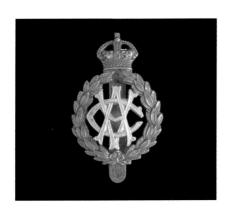

The Army Veterinary Corps

The AVC was responsible for the care of all animals, particularly horses, which were mobilised for war alongside their human colleagues, this Corps wore a bimetal badge comprising the monogram AVC in a wreath, with a crown. An all-brass, but still voided, version of the badge appeared in 1916. Two-and-a-half million horses were treated by the corps in the First World War, a huge effort.

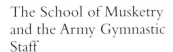

The School of Musketry and the Army Gymnastic Staff

Both specialist units were engaged in training the army. The School of Musketry wore crossed rifles beneath a crown, in brass. The Army Gymnastic Staff wore crossed swords beneath a crown, in brass. Both are illustrated.

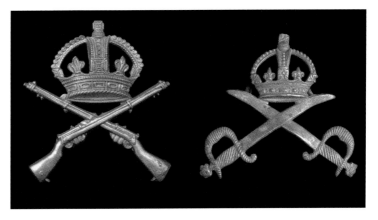

The Non-Combatant Corps

Raised in 1915, the Non-Combatant Corps was composed mostly of conscientious objectors willing to serve in the King's uniform while not bearing arms. It was raised to provide labour both at home and overseas and wore a simple brass badge like a shoulder title, with the monogram NCC; it was worn in the Second World War too.

WOMEN'S SUPPORT SERVICES

In addition to nursing (nurses then did not wear cap badges, *per se*), the following services were raised.

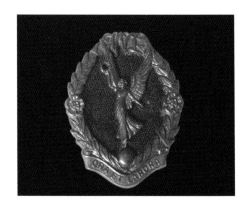

The Women's Legion

The Women's Legion was raised in 1915 to provide support services in a wide range of roles. Its members wore the badge illustrated (with pin fastening), in bronze. Various roles were indicated by the use of coloured enamels or badge backings. This colour indicates the Motor Transport section.

The Women's Army Auxiliary Corps and Queen Mary's Army Auxiliary Corps

The Corps was raised in 1917 to bring women into the army, to serve overseas. Its badge was the simple monogram WAAC in brass, and there are both voided and solid versions. In May 1918 Queen Mary became Colonel-in-Chief, and there was a consequent change in title and badge design, with voided and solid brass versions known.

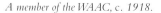

A member of the WAAC, c. 1918.

FURTHER READING

BOOKS

Alderton, G. L. D. *Cap-badges of the British Army 1939–1945*. Spellmount, Staplehurst, 2007.

Anon. *Service Medals, Ribbons, Badges and Flags*. George Philip and Son, London, 1917.

Barnes, Major R. M. *A History of the Regiments and Uniforms of the British Army*. Seeley, Service & Co, 1957.

Barnes, Major R. M. *The British Army of 1914*. Seeley, Service & Co, 1968.

Bodsworth, J. *British Uniforms and Equipment of the Great War, 1914–18. Vol. I. Clothing and Necessaries*. MLRS, 2010.

Bull, S. *World War One British Army. Brassey's History of Uniforms*. Brassey, 1998.

Churchill, C. *History of the British Army Infantry Collar Badge*. Naval & Military Press, Uckfield, 2002.

Cox, R. H. W. *Military Badges of the British Empire 1914–18*. The Standard Art Book Co, Chicago, 1983.

Doyle, P. *Tommy's War. British Military Memorabilia, 1914–1918*. Crowood, Marlborough, 2008.

Doyle, P. *The British Soldier of the First World War*. Shire, Oxford, 2008.

Edwards, D., and Langley, D. *British Army Proficiency Badges*. Wardley Publishing, Frome, 1984.

Edwards, Major T. J. *Badges of HM Services*. Briggs & Co, Manchester, 1943.

Edwards, Major T. J. *Regimental Badges*. Gale & Polden, Aldershot, first edition 1951.

French, D. *Military Identities. The Regimental System, the British Army and the British People c.1870–2000*. Oxford University Press, 2005.

Gaylor, J. *Military Badge Collecting*. Seeley, Service & Co, revised edition 1977.

Hodges, R. *British Army Badges*. Published by the author, 2005.

James, E. A. *British Regiments 1914–18*. Naval & Military Press, Heathfield, fifth edition, 1998.

Jarmin, K. W. *Military 'Sweetheart' Brooches*. Published by the author, 1981.

Kenyon, Lieutenant-Colonel Sir F. *War Graves. How the Cemeteries Abroad Will Be Designed*. HMSO, 1918.

Kipling, A. L., and King, H. L. *Head-dress Badges of the British Army. Volume 1. Up To the End of the Great War*. Naval & Military Press Ltd, Uckfield, 2006.

Kipling, A. L., and King, H. L. *Head-dress Badges of the British Army. Volume 2. From the End of the Great War to the Present Day*. Naval & Military Press Ltd, Uckfield, 2006.

Ward, A. *British Army Cap Badges of the Twentieth Century*. Crowood, Marlborough, 2007.

Westlake, R. *Collecting Metal Shoulder Titles*. Leo Cooper, revised edition, 1996.

Westlake, R. *Kitchener's Army*. Spellmount, Staplehurst, 2003.

Wilkinson, F. *Badges of the British Army. An Illustrated Reference Guide for Collectors*. Arms & Armour Press, 1969.

Wilkinson-Latham, R. J. *Discovering British Military Badges and Buttons*. Shire, Aylesbury, 1973.

WEBSITES

www.1914-1918.net (Excellent and informative)

www.greatwarforum.com (Excellent discussion forum)

www.bmbf.co.uk (Forum for badge collectors and enthusiasts)

ARTICLES

Martin, E. J. 'Badges of Kitchener's army', *Journal of the Society of Army Historical Research*, 21, 124–8; 1942.

Martin, E. J. 'Badges of the Territorial infantry battalions 1908–1922', *ibid*, 22, 57–62; 1943.

Martin, E. J. 'Women's war work with the Army', *ibid*, 25, 54–65; 1945.

Martin, E. J. 'Badges of the London Regiment 1908–1937', *ibid*, 26, 1–10; 1946.

Martin, E. J. 'Badges of Kitchener's army', *ibid*, 35, 35–36; 1957.

Wounded men at the 3rd General Hospital, Le Treport, c. 1917. All present wear caps or slouch hats with their 'hospital blue' uniform. A wide range of cap badges is represented here, including those of the: Australian Imperial Force, Essex Regiment, Gordon Highlanders, Hampshire Regiment, King's Liverpool Regiment, Machine Gun Corps, Middlesex Regiment, North Staffordshire Regiment, Rifle Brigade, Royal Army Medical Corps, Royal Fusiliers, Royal Irish Rifles, Royal Warwickshire Regiment, Royal Welsh Fusiliers, Royal West Kents, South Wales Borderers, and Worcestershire Regiment.

INDEX

Page numbers in italic refer to illustrations